PRAISE FOR F.O.R.G.E.D.

I'm a huge fan of the metaphors in F.O.R.G.E.D. because being able to temper attributes like patience and persistence is key to thriving in business.

DAVID MELTZER—CO-FOUNDER OF SPORTS 1 MARKETING, BEST-SELLING AUTHOR, AND TOP BUSINESS COACH

A unique blend of real-life stories and research, F.O.R.G.E.D. hits the mark with six practices for leaders in current times. I enjoyed the journey from large corporations to a local philanthropy through the lens of learning, transformation and persistence.

FABIENNE JACQUET—DISRUPTIVE INNOVATOR, PH.D., SPEAKER, AUTHOR OF *VENUS GENIUS*

F.O.R.G.E.D. is a concise and enjoyable read in the vein of Mark Schwartz's A Seat at the Table with anecdotal stories and interviews to support the points.

ROQUE MARTINEZ, CHIEF TECHNOLOGY OFFICER, SMARTSTREAM RDU

F.O.R.G.E.D. weaves important research and thought leadership into our current volatile times. It will resonate with any leader or professional who reads this book—as we have all had to adapt to the volatile times that COVID presented to us.

SHARON-LAMM HARTMAN—CEO OF INSIDE-OUT LEARNING, INC. AND AUTHOR OF THE *AUTHENTICITY CODE*

In a time where consistent leadership evolution is critical to the sustained success of every brand and individual, F.O.R.G.E.D. offers a powerful set of mindful and insightful "smithing" tools for new and established leaders alike to effectively embark or continue trekking on their personal growth journeys. Each anecdote and story perfectly illustrates essential life wisdom followed by quick, practical ways to help navigate and courageously manage the beautiful chaos that is leadership. This book is for anyone seeking to humbly be shaped and forged into a better leader, while compassionately helping others do the same.

MIRI RODRIGUEZ—CEO OF MINDFUL LEADERSHIP, AUTHOR OF *BRAND STORYTELLING* AND STORYTELLER AT MICROSOFT CORPORATION

In F.O.R.G.E.D., Dr. Scherer invites us to examine and challenge our notions of what makes us transformative leaders. Many moments in this book remind me of Tolkien's Fellowship of The Rings, written during and for the era of Covid pandemics and beyond. How do we find the courage to surrender ourselves to the fires of change? What will it take for leaders to become resilient, not only to bounce back but bounce back better? How do we cultivate the capability to embrace paradoxes? These are the questions that came up in my mind as I read the stories in this book. I am inspired and humbled at the same time.

DR. HOME NGUYEN, ED.D.—FOUNDER AND MANAGING PARTNER AT MINDKIND INSTITUTE, FACULTY AT COLUMBIA UNIVERSITY, DEPARTMENT OF ORGANIZATIONAL LEADERSHIP

F.O.R.G.E.D.

F.O.R.G.E.D.

SIX PRACTICES OF GREAT LEADERS IN VOLATILE TIMES

*To Carmela —
an amazing F.O.R.G.E.D.
leader. I'm so lucky
to have you as a friend for
all these years.*

DOUGLAS SCHERER

NEW DEGREE PRESS

COPYRIGHT © 2021 DOUGLAS SCHERER

All rights reserved.

F.O.R.G.E.D.

Six Practices of Great Leaders in Volatile Times

ISBN	978-1-63730-676-5	*Paperback*
	978-1-63730-765-6	*Kindle Ebook*
	979-8-88504-041-9	*Ebook*

To My Brilliant and Beautiful Daughter Juliana.

TABLE OF CONTENTS

INTRODUCTION 15
PREFACE 21

PART I.   HOW WE GOT HERE 25
CHAPTER 1. WHY NOW. 27
CHAPTER 2. THE FOUNDRY OF LEARNING. 39
CHAPTER 3. FROM DISRUPTION TO RESILIENCE. 51

PART II.   THE F.O.R.G.E.D. LEADER PRACTICES . . . 73
CHAPTER 4. **F**AVOR COMPASSION. 75
CHAPTER 5. **O**WN THE UNEXPECTED. 91
CHAPTER 6. **R**ECAST IDEAS 103
CHAPTER 7. **G**O WITH INTUITION. 121
CHAPTER 8. **E**MPLOY ACTION COMMUNICATIONS 141
CHAPTER 9. **D**RIVE COMMUNITY BONDS. 157

PART III.   TEMPERING 175
CHAPTER 10. ALTERNATIVE WAYS TO BE A BETTER
            LEADER 177
CHAPTER 11. CONCLUSION 191

GLOSSARY	199
BOOK RELATED WEBSITES	201
ACKNOWLEDGMENTS	203
WORKS CITED	209
INDEX	227

"There are two things that should be the objects of your attention when you are eating a meal. They are the food and the people around you."

—THICH NHAT HANH—YOU ARE HERE

Names and other factual details about individuals, groups, and organizations have been changed, generalized, or omitted in some chapters and stories to protect their privacy. Stories about the author's work experience have been aggregated, and all names changed for similar reasons.

The Antonio Machado stanza in chapter 8 is used per public domain. The English translation by Nélida Quintero is used with the permission of the translator.

INTRODUCTION

Hiking to the Chief Operating Officer's (COO) office required a series of more and more isolating turns that made me wish I'd left a trail of bread crumbs. Legend said he would be tough and threatening.

He greeted me wielding a baseball bat the first time I met him, thus living up to the legend. Grimacing staff members bookended his desk, and it was an even bet whether he was going for bizarre levity or terror. When he spoke, he leaned over his desk, stressing it as the only physical barrier between me and an untimely end. One of my staff members met me there. She whispered her worry.

I had entered *The Forge*.

The Forge is where we transform into leaders at the time of high-impact and ambiguous situations—situations I call *volatile*. The moment can be intimate, like a tough personal decision, or expansive like a worldwide pandemic. Whether you're the defined leader of a group or one who steps up when needed, passing through the Forge of volatile situations transforms you.

The Forge is fickle. One time it might appear as an ill-defined meeting with a terrifying COO. Another it might materialize as a disruptive technology. It can sometimes move quickly like a wildfire that unexpectedly changes direction with a sudden wind or slowly like the growth of a majestic redwood.

As I later learned, the COO's internal team had built a system to track requests flowing into his office. Unfortunately, a year later, they had still not found a way to efficiently report or keep track of those requests.

In the end, we built the COO a great solution. It turned out he and his staff had created sketches of how the screens and reports should look. Since the data he needed was already in the system, his own Information Technology (IT) department was able to build what he wanted. He was so pleased he went around the company saying what a great help I was.

Though the system got upgraded, it was unfortunate his threatening style had lengthened resolution time. He'd worked hard on that tough image, and he filled it well. Even his own IT department was scared to speak with him. When I finally heard his concerns, I quickly realized he didn't have a technology problem.

He simply could not be heard above the noise of his own image.

I connected with the COO simply through listening. Listening is learning. Learning what he needed created a personal connection allowing us to clearly discuss his needs and create an appropriate solution. Since this approach was so effective in building a productive and trusting relationship, let's look at how it can guide team engagement and the bottom line.

> **Note:** I refer to people who practice the six Forged practices described in this book as *Forged leaders*. More specifically, I refer to the Forged leaders interviewed for this book as *Forged interviewees*.

Several of the Forged interviewees had taken new jobs right before the COVID-19 pandemic shutdown started. Thrust into the unfamiliar world of one hundred percent remote work, they led teams they'd never met in person. It was an unanticipated welcome to a new form of working together while apart.

Leaders influence how connected their teams feel. Javier Figueroa-González researched 205 employees at a pharmaceutical manufacturing location. He found they were more engaged in their work, felt safer, and were even more productive when their leaders supported creativity and personal connection over optimized systems and processes.[1,2,3]

1　Javier Figueroa-González, "Manager's Leadership Styles and Employee Engagement: Quantifying Manager's Influence," PhD, Capella University, 2011.

2　William A. Kahn, "Psychological Conditions of Personal Engagement and Disengagement at Work," *The Academy of Management Journal* 33, no. 4 (1990): 692–724.

3　Douglas R. May, Richard L. Gilson, and Lynn M. Harter, "The Psychological Conditions of Meaningfulness, Safety and Availability and the Engagement of the Human Spirit at Work." *Journal of Occupational and Organizational Psychology* 77 (2004): 11–37.

That study tells the story. Leadership efforts that focus on people and creativity can pay off more than process improvement alone. They can help you meet your metrics and be more productive and do so while making your environments more supportive and engaging places to work.

With a foundation in personal connection, the work of Forged leaders expresses their leadership values. Volatile times require this kind of dedication and interaction, as you'll see in the Forged interviewee stories.

THE F.O.R.G.E.D. ACRONYM

Forged leaders take many forms. They can be members of the board of directors, leaders of a small food bank, parents making tough decisions for the family, and individuals making life choices. Each letter in the F.O.R.G.E.D. acronym represents one of the six Forged leader practices as shown below. I provide a short-hand description of the practices in the preface and present them in more detail in chapter 1.

- **F**avor Compassion
- **O**wn the Unexpected
- **R**ecast Ideas
- **G**o with Intuition
- **E**mploy Action Communications
- **D**rive Community Bonds

In my work of teaching, consulting, and researching leadership, I've repeatedly seen that learning and curiosity are core traits for leaders in extreme conditions. Why? Because leaders need to access their skills and experience and apply them to the situation unfolding before them. As Forged leaders, they bring their mettle—what they're made of when the consequences are large—and become vulnerable enough to be shaped by the forge's heat.

·————·✦·————·

A few months into the COVID-19 pandemic, I was working on a book about mindfulness and disruptive leadership. My friend and colleague Fabienne Jacquet, author of *Venus Genius,* invited me to join her writers' cohort at the Creator Institute. Led by Eric Koester, the program emphasizes writing based on interviews and storytelling. I shifted gears immediately. What a perfect time to understand leadership through the stories being lived right in the moment.

What became increasingly clear with each of this book's interviews was that we need people who lead through connection over hierarchy and who navigate by their strengths and experience. These are the Forged leaders I explore in this book. They are the type of leaders I teach about to my students and role models I aspire to emulate.

These ideas grow in importance as we face high-impact challenges. The leaders spotlighted in this book get it, and their stories will help you understand the six Forged leader practices so you can strengthen your Forged leader within.

PREFACE

Here's a quick road map to the book so you can find the parts you like more easily. You can read this book from cover to cover, in any direction, or pick chapters completely out of order.

The three parts of the book move from more theoretical in part one to more narrative in parts two and three.

Part one: How We Got Here—sets the theoretical foundation for parts two and three using stories and case studies as examples.

- Chapter 1: Why Now—Speaks to the importance of the six Forged leadership practices and provides short case examples. Most importantly, this chapter provides the descriptions of each of the Forged practices.
- Chapter 2: The Foundry of Learning—Develops the view that learning reinforces leading in new and fast-moving situations.

- Chapter 3: From Disruption to Resilience—Offers a way to position diverse ideas about disruption within the scope of the six Forged practices.

Part two: The F.O.R.G.E.D. Leader Practices—spotlights one Forged practice in each chapter. The stories were developed by interviewing leaders specifically for this book and matching the story to its most compelling Forged practice.

- Chapter 4: Favor Compassion—Critical encounters where caring won the day.
- Chapter 5: Own the Unexpected—Faced with a surprise that upended everything, these leaders thrived.
- Chapter 6: Recast Ideas—Taking action to bring crucial change by thinking and responding differently in the moment.
- Chapter 7: Go with Intuition—Life and death decisions with help from expertise and gut sense.
- Chapter 8: Employ Action Communications—Leader stories that settle the question "What speaks louder than words?" and why that question is imperative.
- Chapter 9: Drive Community Bonds—Building and supporting your group is everything.

Part three: Tempering—Closes out the book with some alternative and mindfulness techniques for leadership and a call to action.

- Chapter 10—Alternative Ways to Be a Better Leader—Some exploration in opening toward innovation and ease.
- Chapter 11—Conclusion—A quick wrap-up and a final challenge.

Before you start, here are two terms often used in the book that are further described in chapter 1.

- Volatile Times: Moments that require decisions based on only a little information, when the outcome of those decisions and associated actions have a high impact on people's lives.
- Forged Leaders: Individuals called to lead during volatile times.

You're now ready to begin your Forged journey.

PART I

HOW WE GOT HERE

CHAPTER 1

WHY NOW

One night in a busy and crowded city hospital room, a patient wasn't responding. All her vitals looked fine, and she was stable, but something was wrong. The patient would not open her eyes and would not move or speak to any of the nurses or doctors. The medical staff was stumped. What could they be missing? They decided to bring in my friend, a young resident known to be a sharp diagnostician.

"Good afternoon, Ms. X," he said upon entering the room. As before, the patient lay motionless, eyes closed. He reviewed her chart carefully. Nothing stood out as a medical issue in need of additional testing. He looked once more at the information on the chart. The patient's last name appeared to be of Spanish origin, so he decided to try something else.

"Buenas tardes, Señora X."

"Buenas tardes, Doctor!" she exclaimed. Thankful to be feeling so much better, she told him how relieved she was to finally be able to speak. He asked her why she had not spoken to the other doctors. She explained she was being a good patient, quietly letting the doctors do their work. She didn't understand or speak English comfortably, and she did not want to interrupt the medical staff.

In the case of Señora X, culture and language rather than medical complications kept the patient from responding. Doctors and nurses in hospitals work in high-stress situations, literally making life or death decisions. Sometimes the simplest and correct solution may be buried under layers of complex ones. When the resident spoke to Señora X in Spanish, he brought a new cultural perspective to the problem. This type of openness and curiosity opens the Forged leader path.

FORGED LEADERS
Forging is the process of treating metals. A 1918 book by John Jernberg gives a wonderful overview. It's more complicated than you might imagine. Forges can reach over 2,000 degrees Fahrenheit. The metal gets worked through the application of pressure, the pounding of hammers, heat treatment, and shaping and reshaping. This imagery works well as a metaphor for the process leaders go through when they encounter extreme challenges.

As a Forged leader, you are at once the swordsmith and the sword.

The metaphor breaks down in one key area. Jernberg notes you lose your previous work when you reheat metal. He says, "…it should be remembered that when steel has to be heated for subsequent hardening, the effect of all the previous refining is obliterated."[4] Unlike reheated metal, though, Forged leaders take their refinements and experience with them. They use them and change them as needed for each situation. Rather than obliterating a previous refinement, they gain new perspectives with each pass through the forge.

Your Forged leader evolution begins the first time you enter the heat. Each subsequent pass hones you, and you emerge with a slightly different shape and strength. A swordsmith works metal into swords. As a Forged leader, you are at once the swordsmith and the sword. You commit to the challenges of the fire, the openness to be creative, and the willingness to be changed. You emerge different yet whole.

CAPTAIN SULLY SULLENBERGER—"WE'RE GONNA BE IN THE HUDSON."

Each incident of leading in times when a decision can dramatically change the course of a situation increases your capacity to deal with the next cycle through the forge. When Captain Sully Sullenberger landed an Airbus A320 aircraft full of passengers on the Hudson River in 2009, it was a fast decision built upon a long history of experience.

His expertise grew from thirty years as a commercial pilot and twenty as an Air Force pilot and instructor. While in the Air Force, he served as a member of an aircraft accident investigation board and as a mission commander in red flag

---

4 John Jernberg, *Forging; Manual of Practical Instruction in Hand Forging of Wrought Iron, Machine Steel, and Tool Steel; Drop Forging; and Heat Treatment of Steel, Including Annealing, Hardening, and Tempering*. Chicago, IL: American Technical Society, 1918.

exercises that brought together pilots from the Air Force, Navy, Army, Marines, and NATO to provide realistic air combat training. When Sullenberger walked into the forge of US Airlines flight C1549, he brought with him over fifty years of flying experience.

Two minutes and seventeen seconds after their 3:24 p.m. (15:24:54) clearance for takeoff from La Guardia, flight C1549's engines received irrecoverable damage when the plane, carrying 150 passengers and five crewmembers, collided with a flock of geese. Moments later, copilot Jeff Skiles opened to the Emergency Dual Fail Checklist section of the *Quick Reference Handbook* (QRH).

Recording from the Intra-Cockpit Communication:[5]

- 15:27:11: whoa
- 15:27:11.4: [sound of thump/thud(s) followed by shuddering sound]
- 15:27:12: oh #
- 15:27:13: oh yeah [sound similar to decrease in engine noise/frequency begins]
- 15:27:14: uh oh
- ...
- 15:27:28: get the QRH [Quick Reference Handbook] loss of thrust on both engines.

---

5   National Transportation Safety Board, *Aircraft Accident Report: Loss of Thrust in Both Engines after Encountering a Flock of Birds and Subsequent Ditching on the Hudson River US Airways Flight 1549 Airbus A320-214, N106US Weehawken, New Jersey, January 15, 2009,* National Transportation Safety Board (Washington, DC: May 4, 2010), 169–172.

"Get the QRH." Get the playbook containing prescribed steps to follow when faced with a dual engine failure. After several attempts to follow the QRH instructions to restart the engines and review potential solutions with the control tower, Sullenberger and Skiles determined they needed to design their own solution. The only option... attempt to land the plane on the Hudson River.

Recording from Air-Ground Communication[6]

- 15:29:25: we can't do it.
- ...
- 15:29:28: we're gonna be in the Hudson
- 15:29:33: I'm sorry, say again, Cactus?
- ...
- 15:30:09: two one zero uh forty-seven eighteen. I think he said he's goin' in the Hudson

Sullenberger and Skiles made a unique, critical, and correct choice while the airplane was descending at a rate similar to an elevator dropping two stories every second.

At that moment, the two pilots threw out the playbook and made a decision based on their many years of knowledge, experience, and situational awareness. They observed the big picture and quickly calculated how much altitude they had. The higher you are, the farther you can glide. They would have needed a lot of altitude to try for a runway at any airport.

---

6   National Transportation Safety Board, Aircraft Accident Report, 2010, 179–183.

They owned that moment with awareness and skill. A water landing is treacherous. Had Sullenberger dropped a wing during touchdown, the plane would have spun or cartwheeled, ripping it into pieces. Ultimately, their decision for a water landing, along with the rallied crew and passengers themselves, saved the lives of everyone on board.

CEO MARY BARRA—"WE'RE GOING TO FIX THIS."

Extraordinary times seem to find leaders as often by surprise as by design. Captain Sullenberger didn't set out on flight C1549 with the intent of landing on the Hudson. Similarly, Mary Barra didn't expect that a mere three months into her tenure as Chief Executive Officer (CEO) at General Motors (GM), she'd be saddled with the recall of close to a million vehicles for ignition switches that potentially caused fires. These were in addition to the 1.62 million recalls for cars made in 2007 and earlier. By then, faulty ignition switches were the cause of fires that took thirteen lives.[7]

Soon after Barra's appointment, GM engineers brought the issue forward. In response, she acknowledged mistakes had been made and chose to do the right thing: get the message out there and issue a recall. In a 2017 interview at Stanford University, Barra offered key points of working with surprises that speak to all emergencies. "You don't get to choose when you have a crisis. You deal with it now because that's just the way the world works."[8]

---

7   Bill Vlasic and Matthew L Wald, "G.M. Expands Ignition Switch Recall to Later Models," *The New York Times* (New York, NY), March 29, 2014, B1, 4.

8   Ibid.

NEW PLAYBOOK/NEW LANGUAGE

Before her role as CEO, Barra held multiple roles over thirty years of employment at GM. Had Barra ever experienced a massive recall crisis that found her testifying to the United States Congress? No, but she found her way through that new situation based on her generations-long history in the automotive industry.

For thirty-nine years, Barra's father had been a tool and die maker at Pontiac. Her path to the C-suite started as a hood and fender panel inspector at the age of eighteen. Barra tells us, "I think what it does for a CEO is, it makes you realize every person is not homogeneous. Everyone has different needs. Everyone reacts differently to different motivations."[9] Through values instilled from her family and work, her leadership sensibility as a C-Suite executive at a large organization builds on the appreciation of its individuals' differences.

VOLATILE TIMES

Operating without a playbook requires you to act with extreme awareness. Sullenberger and Skiles didn't have time to document their procedures for landing on the Hudson, but through clear and skilled communication and pulling what was needed from existing procedures (such as bracing the passengers for an emergency landing), they created one in real time.

---

9   Laura Putre, "The Barra Era: A Look Back and What's Ahead for GM," *IndustryWeek*, 2020.

In this book, we'll commonly call these dynamic times of ambiguity, risk, unknowns, and high impact that lead to tough decisions and actions—*volatile times*. Volatile times can run the gamut from leading 155,000 employees across six continents at a company like GM to fast changes required in a local volunteer food pantry when the number of families in need suddenly skyrockets by 428 percent, as happened with the Dobbs Ferry Food Pantry.

I purposefully interviewed the leaders in this book during transformational times. But the lessons they impart come from their full career experiences and lead into the future. As a whole, they paint images of leadership that transcend the bounds of a single dramatic moment and instead support the ability to deal with the new. To be a leader in volatile times means you're open to the challenges and opportunities of changing or throwing out your playbook yet one more time.

•• ──────── •✦• ──────── ••

The advent of the 2019 coronavirus pandemic resulted in extreme feelings of isolation, health risks, threats of eviction, economic consequences, and job loss. As the World Health Organization noted in a COVID-19 impact report, "For most, no income means no food, or, at best, less food and less nutritious food."[10] In less volatile times, we might get away with managing the status quo. But during a pandemic, we're called upon to jump into a Forge raised to its highest temperature and lead without clear guidance.

---

10 Kimberly Chriscaden, "Impact of COVID-19 on people's livelihoods, their health and our food systems: Joint statement by ILO, FAO, IFAD and WHO," World Health Organization, May 26, 2021.

That is the essence of leadership. Finding a way forward when you've come to a situation that requires new thinking and new acting, in ways that no one has led before—coming to a wall no one has ever traversed and determining how to climb it. That essence requires a change of perspective that you cannot undo. Together, the decisions you make and the actions you take are transformative.

To be a leader in volatile times means you're open to the challenges and opportunities of changing or throwing out your playbook yet one more time.

Moving into a Forged leadership style is more about building on your experiences than creating a wholly new existence. Remember, you're forging your existing metal, not going out and buying a new sword. You can also think of the process as a spiraling continuum. You keep cycling back through the forge, but you're not just retracing the same circle. You're enhancing it.

THE SIX FORGED LEADER PRACTICES

The people I interviewed for this book withstood the heat of leadership. They found organizational cohesiveness and success through emphasizing the importance of people and learning above oversight and command. My hope is the leader within you will find connections to their stories that support new ways of exploring how you lead.

Together, their stories revealed the six practices described below.

- **F**avor Compassion
    - Make connections with individuals at a personal level. Wield compassion to rally your teams more deeply, consistently, and productively than with fear.

- **O**wn the Unexpected
    - When confronted with the unexpected, Forged leaders investigate it, knowing they don't yet have an answer and may not come up with the perfect one. Into the Forge you go (perhaps unwillingly), but you are not alone. You have your values, experience, humility, and community. You act out of care for others, and you ask for help when needed.

- **R**ecast Ideas
    - Find innovation through improvisation and flexibility.
    - Volatile times force Forged leaders to push themselves out of habitual ways of thinking to take in new and unexpected perspectives.

- **G**o with Intuition
    - Decision-making in volatile times is still based on information, but no amount of information will give Forged leaders one hundred percent certainty. They decide and act by listening to their gut, values, and experience.

- **Employ Action Communications**
  - Messages create energy and community engagement, but Forged leaders use their own actions as their strongest way to communicate intentions.

- **Drive Community Bonds**
  - Forged leaders abandon the lone cowboy mentality and instead build communities. They know it's not only okay to ask for help, but rather receiving support from the community is imperative for the success of moving through volatile times.

Whether in the emergency room, the cockpit, or the C-suite, these surface again and again as critical leadership practices. Leadership has been tortoise-pacing its way toward these practices for decades. As we'll see in the next chapter, volatile times rouse the hare.

CHAPTER 2

THE FOUNDRY OF LEARNING

A few times a year, I check in with my colleague and friend Julia Sloan. Julia is one of the premier leaders in strategic thinking and is a consultant for global business and government leaders. If you've had the opportunity to read her book *Learning to Think Strategically*, now in its fourth edition, you know how her clear and generous style leaves you informed and supported.

The book makes the important delineation of strategic thinking versus strategic planning. The former is a nonlinear, perhaps chaotic, process of discovering and confirming a strategic problem and the environment, context, and power structures in which it operates. The latter finds solutions to the strategic problem through a more objective, at times more quantitative analysis. I think of strategic thinking as a mind-opening and questioning experience, one that helps define the problem. Strategic planning then is a process that closes in on a specific response to the problem.[11]

A few months before our check-in, I had led a retreat where attendees visited a strategic problem through mindfulness, embodiment, and reflective learning. I spoke about Julia's five critical attributes of strategic thinking: "Imagination, Broad Perspective, Juggle, No Control Over, and Desire to Win."[12]

One of the attendees wanted to know how you balance the desire to win with the other attributes like a broad perspective and not having control over the outcome.

This launched our journey into the unknowns of their strategic problem.

The short answer to the attendee's question from Julia's research:

> It's messy.

Forged leadership contains a significant component of strategic thinking, so we need to appreciate that same messiness. Under the perceived and real pressures of high velocity and impact, Forged leaders find ways to allow for some messiness as they work to understand the situations before them. For example, leaders at the start of the COVID-19 pandemic proceeded with little information to guide them while

---

[11] Julia Sloan, *Learning to Think Strategically*, 4th ed. New York, NY: Routledge, 2020.

[12] Ibid, p.215.

performing under the pressures of a life-threatening disease on a massive scale.

JUMPING INTO THE MESS

I asked Julia a question I'd been saving for our discussion. "Does the desire to win work against the opening to the imagination and new perspectives?" She told me I'd pinpointed one of the hardest things for strategic thinkers—staying open to new perspectives and allowing the collision of different ideas and imagination to simmer and develop into something new, even in the face of pressures to move quickly to a winning answer.

> "What we sought to do," Petraeus informs us, "was constantly to have teams out on the battlefield who were looking for lessons."

As she handed me a copy of the newest edition of her book, we noted how dramatically the cover had changed from the first edition. The first edition showed a Mondrian-like set of boxes, as shown in Figure 2.1, which implies a sense that strategic thinking is a clean step-by-step process you can sequence through to happily come to a clear strategic decision. Just follow these steps and voilà, you've accomplished strategic thinking; on to the next thing.

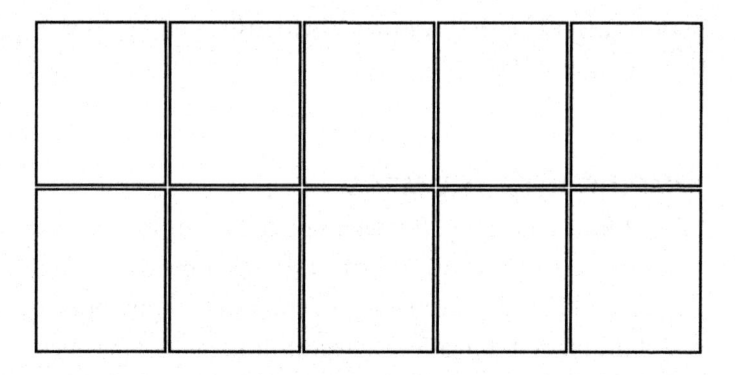

Figure 2.1: Example Similar to the Cover of *Learning to Think Strategically 1st Edition.*

The second and third editions altered the cover only slightly, primarily changing the boxes' color. But the newest cover completely broke the mold, with sweeping brushstrokes whose beginnings and ends are hard to make out. It was immediately clear how the new cover represents the process more accurately.

Julia's book notes there's nothing wrong with linear planning (like the sequential image of boxes in Figure 2.1), but linear plans "are simply insufficient for strategic thinking unless they ride in tandem with [an open mindset]" like the messiness of the splotch in Figure 2.2.[13]

---

13   Ibid, p.28

Figure 2.2: Example Similar to the Cover of
Learning to Think Strategically 4th Edition

The challenge then for Forged leaders and strategic thinkers is staying within the realm of questioning your assumptions about the problem, even when all hell breaks loose.

President Dwight D. Eisenhower hit it right on the head in his address to the 1957 National Defense Executive Reserve Conference. "Plans are worthless, but planning is everything. There is a very great distinction because when you are planning for an emergency, you must start with this one thing. The very definition of an emergency is that it is unexpected. Therefore it is not going to happen the way you are planning."[14] While the process of planning provides insight and preparedness, you may never use the plan in the precise way it was designed.

---

14 Dwight D. Eisenhower, *Public Papers of the Presidents of the United States, Dwight D. Eisenhower, 1957: Containing the Public Messages, Speeches, and Statements of the President, January 1 to December 31, 1957*, College Park, MD: General Services Administration, National Archives and Records Service, Federal Register Division, 1958.

Like strategic thinking, leading in volatile times is a messy process that you can't clean with an unchangeable plan. Labeling it volatile tells you right away this moment of leadership is not like the others. It calls upon you to stay with the messiness and think, ponder, and act in new ways. As we'll see next, this is especially true when you're running a large operation.

•• ———————— •✦• ———————— ••

I was fortunate to participate in a group discussion on leadership with guest speaker General David Petraeus. Among Petraeus's many leadership roles are Commander of the United States Central Command and Director of the Central Intelligence Agency.

One of his key instructions for leaders was to build learning and creative teams and to consistently revisit their strategies to see how they meet each situation. He also spoke about the importance of learning in an interview with the *Belfer Center for Science and International Affairs*.

"What we sought to do," Petraeus informs us, "was constantly to have teams out on the battlefield who were looking for lessons."[15] Each of his commanders was required to bring two new learnings from the battlefield to each of his monthly meetings. "So, we were always emphasizing [that learning] is a key piece of the counterinsurgency field manual." Petraeus had formalized ways throughout his organization to continuously learn.

---

15 David H. Petraeus, "David Petraeus on Strategic Leadership," By Emile Simpson, *Belfer Center for Science and International Affairs*, Belfer Center for Science and International Affairs.

CHANGING PLAYBOOKS

Learning requires the openness to change the way you see things. Petraeus created a learning organization that allowed his commanders to make those changes and examine their extent. "Did we need a change to a field manual, or [create] an entirely new field manual?" This was one of the questions Petraeus opened to his commanders.[16] Similarly, Forged leaders must be willing to throw out the old playbook.

The playbook can be represented by monthly meetings to review and change or replace a field manual. It can also reveal itself during battle, where every speck of your experience feeds into strategic thinking, planning, and acting right in the moment. As we'll see, whether in real-time dynamic situations or larger organizational learning efforts like a siren luring your ship to the rocks, you need to be wary of a hidden deterrent to learning—success.

THE SUCCESS PARADOX

People, businesses, and organizations typically start any project with the idea of succeeding. Success takes all kinds of forms: financial, romantic, personal, organizational, and more. Whichever form, it usually feels great when it happens. Your body loves that experience so much it rewards you with a bit of dopamine to make you feel good. The dopamine effectively brings your attention to the great thing you just did. It can even create new synaptic connections in the area

---

16   Ibid.

of the brain where it was released and lock the event into your memory.[17]

There is nothing wrong with that, except the timing of the dopamine reward changes with repetition. Instead of being rewarded after an event is complete, your system begins to release dopamine when it *anticipates* a positive outcome.[18,19] Since you are rewarded for following the same steps that led you to the original and repeated accomplishment, you may be demotivated to try new or different approaches.

One way of challenging this reinforcement of habitual behaviors is by nurturing curiosity. Taking in new information, like reading or simply exploring a new topic, even in the absence of an extrinsic goal like studying for an exam, can act as a reward in itself.[20,21] To me, this highlights the importance of creating a learning environment and maintaining the joy of trying new things—of exploring and innovating.

A few years back, I was skiing at a local family-run mountain in New York. Next to me were a dad and son readying

---

17 Richard C. Deth, *Molecular Origins of Human Attention the Dopamine-Folate Connection*, New York, NY: Springer Science+Business, 2003.

18 Robert M. Sapolsky, *Why Zebras Don't Get Ulcers*, New York, NY: Holt Paperbacks, 2004.

19 "Dopamine Jackpot! Sapolsky on the Science of Pleasure," August 18, 2021. Lecture.

20 Caroline Braun Marvin, "How Curiosity Drives Actions and Learning: Dopamine, Reward, and Information Seeking," Doctor of Philosophy, Columbia University, 2016.

21 Ellen Tedeschi, "Knowledge for the Sake of Knowledge: Understanding the Relationship between Curiosity, Exploration, and Reward" Doctor of Philosophy, Columbia University, 2020.

themselves for the chairlift: a bit of fumbling with gloves, testing whether toes or heels of the boot go first into the binding. Everything was new to the boy going up the mountain for the first time.

Imagine the wonder!

Once both of them were ready, father holding the boy's hand gliding him away toward the lift, I heard the boy ask his dad, "But what if I fall?"

"Falling," replied the dad, "is learning." And off they went.

It's hard to envision a work supervisor responding the same way to the similar question of, "What if I fail?"

"Hey, boss. This project directly affects my annual goals, which directly impacts my annual review, which directly impacts my potential for a salary increase, bonuses, continued employment, and career advancement. What if I fail?"

Even for the best leaders, there's a two-pronged reaction. Part of their reaction trends toward the "falling-is-learning" side. The other part knows their own reward structure is tied to to their team's achievements. This is one reason it could be difficult for direct supervisors to be transformative mentors.[22] They may become reluctant to allow their staff opportunities to try and fail (to learn) since their appraisals are directly

---

22 Douglas Scherer, "Levinson's Dream Theory and Its Relevance in an Academic Executive Mentoring Program: An Exploratory Study of Executive Mentors' Practice and Individuation," Ed.D., Columbia University, 2010.

linked. In that way, their fear of failing can stifle opportunities for curiosity and creativity.

TWO LEADER TYPES

Like General Petraeus, you have to foster learning capabilities in your organization, keep an open mind and think strategically. Nonaka's often-cited study of car manufacturing suggests promoting organizational learning through incentives like promotions and transfers.[23] Unfortunately, once incentives enter the picture, leaders are looped back to quantifying the effort to determine how to disperse the incentives to the team. Next, the success paradox may kick in, and the learning cycle that should unlock creativity instead becomes a closed loop of repetition.

Physicist Fritjof Capra's observations of biology, physics, and social interactions in *The Hidden Connections* begin to loosen the loop. He found a mixture of chaos, communication, and instability fertilizes emergent ideas.[24] Yet building a work environment that fosters innovation through learning and chaos already sounds a bit like trying to capture lightning. Capra helps by defining two types of leaders, traditional and facilitative, which together create an innovative environment.

---

23 Ikujiro Nonaka, "Toward Middle-up-Down Management: Accelerating Information Creation," *Sloan Management Review* 9, no. 3 (1988): 9–18.

24 Fritof Capra, *The Hidden Connections: Integrating the Biological, Cognitive, and Social Dimensions of Life into a Science of Sustainability*, New York, NY: Double Day, 2002.

- **Traditional leaders** serve as a standard of what to strive for in vision, values, and goals.
- **Facilitative leaders** create the conditions that facilitate the emergence of innovation.

Forged leaders endeavor to balance the two types of leadership and pave the way for learning communities and creativity. Whether leading a small team or a large organization, they guide with their values while staying aware and open. The good news is that passing through the Forge is itself a learning process. The stories in this book illustrate that Forged leaders are not just born. They are shaped through learning.

CHAPTER 3

FROM DISRUPTION TO RESILIENCE

One day I found myself in a bobsled, holding on for dear life while screaming 55 miles per hour down the twists and turns of the Olympic run at Lake Placid, New York. Thank goodness one of the three other people in the sled was an experienced bobsled driver.

One of the distinctive things about Lake Placid is its history as an Olympic Village. In 1980, it saw the United States upset win over Russia in ice hockey in what became known as the "Miracle on Ice." They've since taken fantastic advantage of the Olympic infrastructure to offer all kinds of activities.

The region's *Whiteface Mountain* is as much fun to ski as it is gorgeous to see. My daughter knows better than I do since she was on the local ski race team as a kid. Once, we visited the mountain and her day group took her hurtling down the Olympic race trail. Afterward, she joined my wife and me to help us master the beginner and intermediate trails.

While my daughter and I have both plummeted thrillingly at high speeds, there's a big difference. She was taking control of her twists and turns through practice and skill, speeding down the race trail, making split-second decisions based on things like snow conditions, visibility, and skill level. I was just hanging on for dear life.

One of us was a leader.

Hint: It wasn't me.

For spectators, a ski race trail might look pretty much the same throughout the day. But skiers know the trail changes dramatically throughout the race. The runs morph based on things like the skiers' positions in the lineup, changes in weather, differences of shade at specific turns in the morning versus the afternoon, and more.

Leaders constantly experience these types of changes. You can plan for some, but there are still a lot of unknowns until the exact spot and time that you reach them. And *then* you know them. Any one of these changes can disrupt your plan. How you arrive at these unexpected moments, how you interact with and respond to the changing unknowns of the course's landscape, in large part determines your success in that race and your growth as a skier to compete in the next.

DISRUPTION HERALDS THE NEW

Disruption is everywhere. We see it in technological advances like smartphones and self-driving cars, products that changed the landscape of communication and travel.

Technology is not the only thing that disrupts, though. The COVID-19 pandemic shifted our normal way of interacting. It showed up at our door and said, "World, things are going to be different for a while." We often think of disruption as something that throws a large set of people off balance. But disruptions can be local as well, like when a family member is injured or even comes into a surprise inheritance. Essentially, disruption heralds the new.

The word "disruption" reached buzzword status beginning with a doctoral dissertation by Clayton Christensen in 1992. He later leveraged his dissertation into a set of books and products that have been popular and influential from the 1990s until today.

Christensen's research looked at the market for a new computer storage medium, the eight-inch floppy disk drive. He found "the lead architectural innovators" (the disruptors) were unestablished innovative companies. They were "entrants." It's reasonable to think newcomers would be the underdogs since, by definition, they don't yet have an established competitive product.

Not so fast.

They are competitive specifically because they're not tied to the confines and architecture of their past product line. In Christensen's idea, they were able to create a new product design along "nontraditional dimensions."

Here's where the success paradox rubber meets the innovation road. Success is great, no question. But when it locks you onto a track that you are incapable or afraid of jumping off, you innovate only along the path you are already on. You are what Christensen calls an "incumbent."[25,26] Entrants, as opposed to incumbents, do not have an existing track. They can lay new track since they are not tied to earlier successes and designs. They work toward boarding people onto their train, which is going to new places and situations. They toss the old playbook and disrupt.

DISRUPTION VELOCITY

How fast does disruption happen? Conflicting theories seem to point in multiple directions. Is it something that changes the landscape forever with speed and power, or does it grow slowly, taking over all challengers, like a neighbor's ivy invading your lawn?

The answer to this conflict is yes.

Christensen's dissertation concludes that disruption is not a sudden wow and fade. Rather, it exists when innovative architecture retains its "positions of industry leadership across

---

25 Clayton M. Christensen, "The Innovator's Challenge: Understanding the Influence of Market Environment on Processes of Technology Development in the Rigid Disk Drive Industry," Doctor of Business Administration Dissertation, Harvard University, 1992.

26 Arpan Yagnik and Yamini Chandra. "Using Creativity to Defeat Fear and Manage Ambiguity for Enhancing Entrepreneurial Decisions," In *The Anatomy of Entrepreneurial Decisions: Past, Present and Future Research Directions*, edited by Andrea Caputo and Massimiliano M. Pellegrini, Contributions to Management Science, 9–28, Cham, Switzerland: Springer Nature, 2019.

generations of architectural technologies."[27] You enter the playing field with something new, and you grow into a leader.

Other theories consider disruption to be a *Big Bang*.

Big Bang is especially strong in this era of big data and machine learning. In Big Bang, incumbents attempt to predict the next market shift through big data analytics. Then they take sweeping and swift action, like integrating lower-cost innovations into their existing product line. The idea is this strategy will help them elude misfortunes that befell Toys "R" Us and Blockbuster.[28,29]

Disruption and Big Bang theories help explain how businesses stay relevant and competitive. Yet, those theories continue to evolve with changing business environments. It may be suitable then to think of the topic in a new way, through resilience.

RESILIENCE—THE NEW DISRUPTION

When I attended the Mindful Leader Summit held in Washington DC, topics ranged from working with individual trauma to heightening group performance. By chance, I sat

---

27 "Disruption 2020: An Interview with Clayton M. Christensen," MIT Sloan Management Review, 2020, accessed September 10, 2021. P. 112.

28 Jacques Bughin and Nicolas van Zeebroeck, "The Case for Offensive Strategies in Response to Digital Disruption." iCite-International Centre for Innovation, Technology and Education Studies, Bruxelles, Belgium, 2017.

29 Downes, Larry and Paul F. Nunes. "Big-Bang Disasters." *Harvard Business Review* March 2013: 44–56.

next to Rebecca Reynolds, an expert in the field of resilience or helping individuals and groups strengthen their ability to adapt to adversity. She has developed programs for executives and workshops for kids.

Overcoming adversity, becoming sustainable and innovative, and surviving and thriving typify resilience. She explained it this way:

> "Transition is slow. Change is often fast."
>
> "People resist change since human nature is to stay with [the way things are].
>
> Transitioning is preparing for [the next thing]."[30]

Through these four notions of transition, change, velocity, and resistance to new things, I began to see resilience as a potential way to bridge the differing theories of the disruptive experience (such as fast, slow, Big Bang). I grouped them into three categories:

- Resilient Transition: Characterized by lower velocity and less resistance
    - Exemplified below through the story of Amazon's early strategy

- Resilient Change: Characterized by higher velocity and greater resistance

---

[30] Rebecca Reynolds, "Discussion on Resilience," By Douglas Scherer, December 7, 2020.

- Exemplified below through the stories of how Kodak and Fujifilm handled the advent of the digital camera
- Resilient Transformation: Characterized by unpredictable velocity and resistance
  - Exemplified below through the story of LEGO Mindstorms

Let's start with a story of resilient transition and a 1997 letter to Amazon shareholders from then CEO Jeff Bezos.

RESILIENT TRANSITION

When viewed in the light of Reynolds's comments (transition is slow, change is fast), Christensen's disruption is more akin to resilient transition. Transition moves slowly. Hence there is likely less resistance to the innovation. Take the floppy disk he used as the basis for his dissertation. Its introduction came before most computers could use it. But as more companies produced computers, more models supported the ability to use a floppy disk.

THE AMAZON LETTER

When Amazon first appeared in the early 1990s, I remember having conversations where people just couldn't understand how Amazon would survive as just another e-commerce vendor. Then, Amazon went public on May 15, 1997, and the questions shifted to how could they continue to exist without a huge profit margin? But the extreme success of Amazon proved the naysayers wrong and showed us how resilient transition acts.

Amazon's initial public offering (IPO) price was eighteen dollars per share. Flash forward twenty-two years and that investment saw a total return of 113,000 percent.[31] Looking at their success might lead you to think they burst onto the scene with a radical, immediate, explosive change idea. But their 1997 annual report opens with a letter to their shareholders that shows they planned a longer fuse from the start.

Bezos, opens by preparing shareholders for his purposeful thought process. Watch how strongly he emphasizes the slow strategy of taking over the market.

"We believe that a fundamental measure of our success will be the shareholder value we create over the *long term*. This value will be a direct result of our ability to extend and solidify our current market leadership position."[32]

Then, once he's laid the foundation of a long-term strategy, he speaks to how he will leverage Amazon's market share to drive revenue.

"The stronger our market leadership, the more powerful our economic model. Market leadership can translate directly to higher revenue, higher profitability, greater capital velocity, and correspondingly stronger returns on invested capital."[33]

---

31   John Ballard, "If You Invested $500 in Amazon's IPO, This Is How Much You'd Have Now," *The Motley Fool* (November 14, 2019).

32   Jeffrey P. Bezos, *Amazon.Com Annual Report—1997*, Amazon.com (Seattle, WA: 1997).

33   Ibid.

The strategy Bezos presents to the shareholders falls directly in line with the characteristics of resilient transition shown in Figure 3.1.

- **Less Resistance:** Bezos was looking to transition retail shopping and initiated a strategy of generating Amazon customer loyalty over time rather than trying to jerk consumers away from their favorite retailers.
- **Slower Paced:** He begins his letter by preparing the shareholders to expect that growth will be a longer cycle. They would not measure success solely in revenue or share price but in a significant part by nurturing customer loyalty.

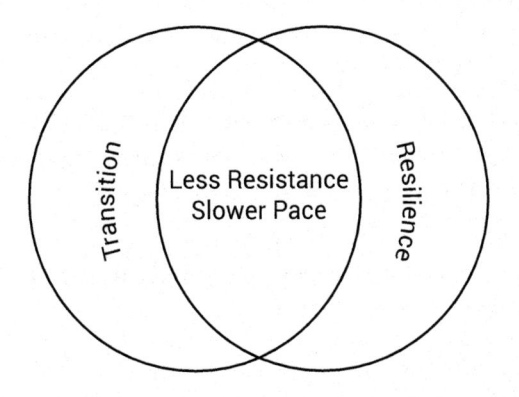

Figure 3.1: Characteristics of Resilient Transition

The Amazon case allows us to view Christensen's concept of disruption through the resilient transition lens. In his last interview in November 2019, twenty-eight years after his dissertation, his core definition of disruption had barely changed. "Products and services often appear modest at the outset but over time have the potential to transform an industry."[34]

Resilient Transition describes more the ivy taking over the lawn than it does a Big Bang. It takes a little more time to grow, but when it does, it has fully taken over.

RESILIENT CHANGE

While resilient transition unfolds as a long-term strategy with less resistance, by contrast, resilient change recognizes that something new is here and asks the innovator to make a fast pivot in thought and action to make use of it. But organizations, especially incumbents, tend to have resistance to that kind of fast pivot.[35,36] Reynolds's resilience ideas tell us that high-speed change increases pushback. Without flexibility, leaders find it difficult to move out of their known comfort zones of what already seems to be working. They fall prey to the change rather than traversing or gaining from it. Such was the case at Kodak Corporation with disastrous results.

HAVING IT FIRST

In 1975, twenty-five-year-old engineer Steve Sasson created the prototype of the digital camera in the Kodak Photographic Research Laboratory, which would eventually change the way people took pictures. Then, in 1977, Robert

---

34 Christensen, An Interview with Clayton M. Christensen, 2021.
35 Bughin and Van Zeebroeck, The Case for Offensive Strategies in Response to Digital Disruption, 2017.
36 Downes and Nunes, Big-Bang Disasters, 2013.

Shanebrook, Kodak Worldwide Product-Line Manager, prepared an internal report predicting digital cameras would one day surpass film cameras.

He predicted they would be the "camera of the future." In an interview with Kenny Suleimanagich, Shanebrook would later recount how his ideas were received, "Electronic photography was certainly paid attention to by some, but many didn't think much of it."[37]

The C-suite wasn't impressed. They were comfortable with the safe zone of selling film, which provided more immediate gains to the shareholders. And for a short while, doubling down on the habitual way of showing shareholders profit worked. But photographic film sales reached their peak in 2000 and then began their decline to less than a tenth of their peak in 2010. Two years later, the 188-year-old Kodak Corporation filed for bankruptcy.[38,39,40]

The pivot to digital had gone directly against their core competency of film products and processing. The C-suite had little interest in some new-fangled technology with the potential to undermine their profitable areas. They fundamentally

---

37 Kenny Suleimanagich, "The Decline of a Giant: An inside Look at Kodak's Downfall." MS, Columbia University, 2013, p.4.

38 Jonathan C. Ho and Hongyi Chen. "Managing the Disruptive and Sustaining the Disrupted: The Case of Kodak and Fujifilm in the Face of Digital Disruption." *Review of Policy Research* 35, no. 3 (2018): 353–71.

39 Shigetaka Komori, *Innovating out of Crisis: How Fujifilm Survived (and Thrived) as Its Core Business Was Vanishing.* Berkeley, CA: Stone Bridge Press, 2013.

40 Christian Sandströmarchive, "You Press the Button. Kodak Used to Do the Rest." *MIT Technology Review*, 2011.

saw Kodak as a chemical dispensary. In the early 1980s, CEO Colby Chandler gave an interview to the *Rochester Democrat and Chronicle*. When asked about the future for Kodak over the next twenty-five to fifty years, he planted his feet firmly in the past. "Kodak's work has always been with the miracle of the molecule."[41]

Kodak effectively gave the entire digital camera game away by sticking to the past with film and trying to give short-term gains to the stockholders. Instead of getting behind their new technology, they simply licensed the Kodak name to Flextronics to produce their digital photography line.[42] Christensen summed up the Kodak story. "I guess what we have to learn from Kodak is that the language and the way of thinking need to go all the way to the Board. At Kodak, the process was left to subsequent CEOs, and the old financial way of thinking crept back into the company."[43] Kodak did not make the pivot, but a different photography company did.

MAKING IT HAPPEN

Like Kodak, Fujifilm was also in the business of photographic film. But Fujifilm made the pivot to restructure its business to incorporate digital photography rather than just farming it

---

41 Suleimanagich, The Decline of a Giant: An inside Look at Kodak's Downfall, p.6.

42 James Euchner and Clayton M. Christensen. "Managing Disruption: An Interview with Clayton Christensen," *Research Technology Management* 54, January–February 2011, no. 1 (2011): 11–17.

43 Ibid, p.17.

out. They developed the technology in-house and controlled the development and production of their digital cameras.[44]

By 2000, when color film sales peaked, Fujifilm had already surpassed film sales of Kodak. But Shigetaka Komori, then Fujifilm President, saw the market changing away from film and made the pivot.

When Komori tells the story, it just makes sense. "It soon became clear we would preside in our leadership over a contracting market. Digital cameras were already spreading like wildfire, basically eliminating the need for film."[45]

Komori's instinct proves far more than just a realization the market was going to pass Fujifilm. Komori has an underlying philosophy that underscores his awareness and flexibility. "In an often unpredictable business world," Komori tells us, "a peak always conceals a treacherous valley."[46] While Kodak seemed to ignore the valley where their film-parachute landing was heading, Komori and Fujifilm were already scaling the next peak.

Komori's sense of the market and ability to pivot propelled Fujifilm to beat Kodak in the digital camera market and is a great example of how to work with resilient change shown in Figure 3.2.

---

44 Ibid.
45 Komori, Innovating out of Crisis, 2013, p.19.
46 Ibid.

- **More Resistance:** While resilient change leads to more resistance, Komori came into the game with an openness to change. He recognized and respected change had come, and while he didn't abandon Fujifilm's core competency in the film market, he did make an assessment of the future and pivoted toward it. Rather than fear or resist, he understood and entered the new market.
- **Faster Paced:** When faced with the fast pace of change, some individuals and organizations begin to resist, perhaps falling back on their past ways of acting. Instead, Komori opened to the challenge when he developed his own road map where there was none.

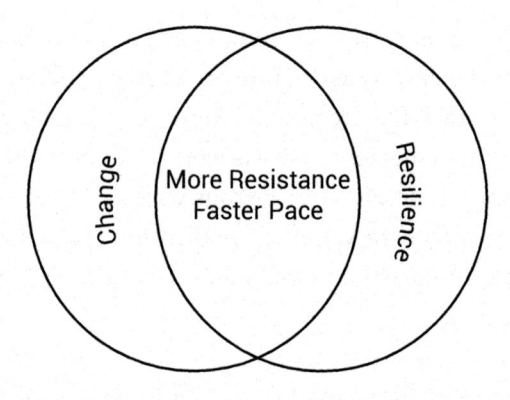

Figure 3.2: Characteristics of Resilient Change

It's critical you are observant and open to the future once it's recognized so you can decide if and how you want to move toward it. Sometimes it's not clear which direction to pivot. For LEGO, their customers unveiled that direction.

RESILIENT TRANSFORMATION

The Kodak story shows that resistance arises as a reaction when vast opportunity accompanies a dramatic change, thus inhibiting the ability to take advantage of the change. Transitions burn more slowly, yet as seen in the case of Amazon, they begin with a strategic focus for long-term action supported by a mix of dedication and belief.

A third type of resilience, resilient transformation, performs more like an unpredictable wildfire. Without warning, it appears, changes direction with a sudden shift in the wind, demands an immediate response, and has the potential for huge impact. The success of LEGO Mindstorms tells that story.

The LEGO story begins in 1932 when master carpenter Ole Kirk Kristiansen began making wooden toys for children. He incorporated the business with the name LEGO three years later. The LEGO name was formed from the two words Leg Godt, meaning "play well." The introduction of the original version of LEGO interlocking bricks came in 1949.

In volatile times it's hard to know if you're at the beginning of a change cycle or passing through a transition with active patience. The only thing for certain is if you think things are permanent, you are in for a shock.

Nearly three-quarters of a century after Ole Kirk Kristiansen began making toys, three events intertwined and triggered LEGO into an unplanned state of transformational soul searching. They had to make a key decision that balanced proprietary ownership and community engagement. Would LEGO make the right decision?

EVENT 1: LEGO MINDSTORMS

The first event occurred in January 1998 when LEGO unveiled its Mindstorms product line of programmable bricks at the Royal College of Art in London. The Robotic Command Explorer (RCX) programmable brick could give instructions to a robot built of LEGO components. Sensor bricks further allowed the LEGO robots to react to environmental stimuli like physical objects or sunlight. You could program the robot, for example, to stop when it bumped into a wall.

LEGO followed with an official launch of RCX in September 1998. By December 1 Mindstorms was sold out.[47] The movement toward Mindstorms had been going on since 1984 when Kjeld Kirk Kristiansen, then LEGO's CEO, visited Massachusetts Institute of Technology (MIT) Artificial Intelligence Laboratory to find out more about Seymour Papert's programmable robotic turtle. Papert cofounded the laboratory in the 1960s and, with a worldwide team, developed the Logo programming language as a creative learning tool. The turtle received its walking orders through Logo commands while wired to a computer. Fourteen years later, Mindstorms operated free of computer wires.

RCX is controlled through the published LEGO/Logo programming language designed at the MIT laboratory. As a

---

47 "Lego Mindstorms: A History of Educational Robots." Hack Education, Updated December 13, 2020.

proprietary measure, LEGO had not exposed the brick's internals. For RCX enthusiasts, that challenge led to the second event: finding a way to access the RCX internals and gain more programmatic control over the robot.

I participated in an authors' group discussion with guest speaker Simon Sinek, who writes and presents on optimism through the context of knowing "your WHY" or purpose.[48] One of his key tools revolves around his notion of the golden circle. The center of the circle is where you find the WHY that inspires you.

> "We came to understand that limiting creativity is the opposite of our mission."

Sinek talked about the importance he gives to inventing the right language to speak with people and create a connection. Yet, when he invents a language as he did with the golden circle, he does not trademark it. He was asked in the authors' group why he does not legally protect it? "I don't want to be the only one who talks about it and does it. I want everybody to use it. That's what makes it spread."[49] The idea of making it spread was about to compel LEGO to explore their own Why.

---

48 Sinek, Simon. *Start with Why: How Great Leaders Inspire Everyone to Take Action.* New York, NY: Portfolio/Penguin, 2009, p.79.

49 "Simon Sinek," By Eric Koester, *Creator Institute*, Creator Institute.

EVENT 2: HACKING THE BRICK

Almost immediately after the RCX 1998 release, Keoko Proudfoot, an Engineering Masters graduate from Stanford University, presented a paper at the University's EE380 annual conference titled, "Reverse Engineering the LEGO RCX." The paper exposed much of the brick's internal design.

He writes, "While the RCX is certainly a fun and useful product out-of-box, it is even more exciting under the hood. Reverse engineering has revealed enough details about the machine it is now possible to escape the limitations of the standard programming environment."[50] Proudfoot had just shown the inner workings of RCX to the world. LEGO enthusiasts could now program the brick beyond its intended and proprietary design. This set the stage for the final event.

EVENT 3: THE PIVOT

In an effort to get control over hackers, the US government legislated The Digital Millennium Copyright Act of 1998 (DMCA), which was signed into law by President Bill Clinton on October 28, 1998.[51] The DCMA, in part, criminalized the circumvention (hacking) of devices like the programmable brick. So, when Proudfoot hacked the RCX and published the instructions, LEGO was suddenly in a transformational dilemma.

---

50 "Reverse Engineering the Lego RCX," Kekoa Proudfoot, Updated December 13, 2020.

51 US Copyright Office, "The Digital Millennium Copyright Act of 1998 : US Copyright Office Summary," edited by US Copyright Office, Washington, DC: US Copyright Office, 1998.

Initially, LEGO pursued prosecution under the DMCA. But in a surprise turn, they changed direction and moved toward a model of open innovation where anyone could change the software. What changed their minds? Their values. "We came to understand that limiting creativity is the opposite of our mission," recounted Mads Nipper, the company's marketing chief, in a 2013 interview with *Smithsonian Magazine*.[52]

Like Sinek, LEGO wanted their message to spread, opening the product and ideas to their followers. This move fostered deeper engagement by enthusiasts and middle school programs. The decision reinvigorated the LEGO movement. Their profit margin grew from .8 percent in 1997 to 2.8 percent in 1999.[53] Mindstorms has since become the best-selling LEGO product.[54]

Resilient transformation often arrives as a surprise that forces you to do some deep searching to determine the next move. It plays out in an environment that's out of control. These types of transformations don't limit themselves to technology. They happen in the realms of politics, social transformation, and personal life events.

Given the unknowns in resilient transformation, it can play out with elements from both resilient transition and resilient change, as shown in Figure 3.3.

---

52 Franz Lidz, "How Lego Is Constructing the Next Generation of Engineers," *Smithsonian Magazine* May 2013.
53 LEGO Company, *Annual Accounts 1999*, LEGO (Billund, Denmark: 1999).
54 Lidz, How Lego Is Constructing the Next Generation of Engineers, 2013.

- **Transition:** In the LEGO Mindstorms scenario, the end of a long cycle of development and patents emerges. Cracks form in the certainty of locked down ownership, and the corporate values and mission are revisited for guidance.
- **Change:** Things moved fast and got out of control in 1998. Mindstorms was hacked, and LEGO had to make a decision. Sue the hackers or more deeply engage the LEGO Mindstorms community. A debate ensued between LEGO legal and marketing. They decided to drop the hacking case, and LEGO enthusiasts became even more engaged in the product.[55]

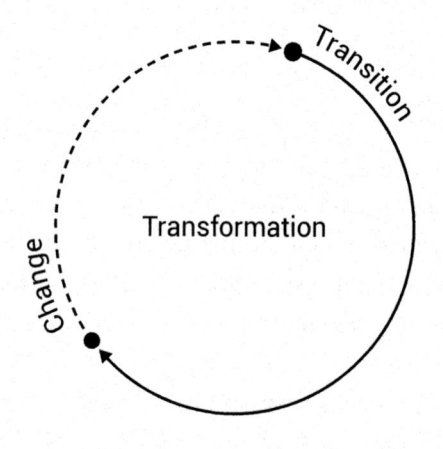

Figure 3.3: The Nature of Resilient Transformation

The "D" in F.O.R.G.E.D. stands for "Drive Community Bonds." And that's exactly what LEGO did. Instead of suing

---

55 Ibid.

their enthusiasts, they engaged them. Like LEGO getting hacked leading to an open innovation model of engaging customers, or the COVID-19 virus unexpectedly taking the world on a pandemic adventure, the way leaders and individuals step up and respond, make decisions, deal with ambiguity, and care for others greatly influences, at times transforms—everyone involved.

SUMMARY

In this chapter, we saw a new way to view disruption through the lens of resilience. Three forms of resilience were identified based on their levels of speed and resistance:

- **Resilient Transition**: Oriented toward the end of a life cycle and a slower journey that's subject to less resistance
- **Resilient Change**: Often positioned more toward the beginning of a life cycle, faster moving and frequently greeted with stronger resistance
- **Resilient Transformation**: Full of unknowns, the life cycle is nudged at the end, beginning or a combination of both, and usually involves a revisit to the driving values and vision

This book's primary focus is on resilient transformation. The Forged interviews show resilient transformation summons a kind of leadership that can respond to those messy and dynamic situations. You have to make decisions knowing there are no perfect choices.

As we'll see, Forged leaders use skillsets that are not necessarily new but must be applied. They are living, growing beings, and as such, the next chapter on Favoring Compassion is a great place to start our journey through the six Forged practices.

PART II

THE F.O.R.G.E.D. LEADER PRACTICES

CHAPTER 4

FAVOR COMPASSION

Greg threw his hands in the air. His technology team told him his idea was too radical and not possible. Discussions over the last three years had reached an impasse. By the time I met Greg in his office, he and his team were locked into an endless loop of exasperation.

Greg was a senior executive who wanted to join statistics from his customer response group with data from other business areas. With that, he'd be able to correlate customer interactions with product availability to improve the customer experience and open opportunities for cross-selling. He didn't demand moving mountains. He simply sought a new and smarter way of visualizing data that already existed in his organization's database.

During my years as an independent consultant, a word-of-mouth reputation developed around my ability to bridge these kinds of executive and technology team jams. It's not a role I purposely developed, yet it turned out to be one I was great at and enjoyed. So it stuck.

Across multiple organizations, one executive after another lamented their own technology teams failed to give them the functionality to do their jobs. Some of the executives even felt oppressed. My work with Greg was one example. His technology team couldn't, or wouldn't, learn the language of his new business ideas. So, he was confined to tell them about his ideas in the language of the existing application's field names and on-screen button choices designed years earlier.

••———————•✦•———————••

A while back, I was fortunate to live in Venice, Italy, for three months. When I first got there, my Italian was pretty bad. "Give me some orange juice, please," I asked in the first salumeria I saw. They handed me an orange soda. At least, I'd ordered something drinkable that tasted kind of orange.

The distance between Greg's new objectives and the old playbook would not have gotten him even that close. His pointing at the screen couldn't show me what he wanted. It was as frozen in time as it was useless. He needed freedom to express himself so, I had to break us out of this language prison. To help him, I brought some compassion to the situation. Together we would find a fresh language.

At times like these, images often speak louder than words.[56] I asked Greg to turn off his screen, forget for a moment about the computer in front of him, and simply draw a picture of what he wanted. Released from the confines of the screen, he started thinking visually onto the page.

---

56   Paulo Freire, *Pedagogy of the Oppressed*, New York: Herder and Herder, 1970.

He was rewriting the playbook.

Our conversation stopped being about database descriptions, canned reports, and technology concerns. It shifted into stories of what he wanted to accomplish, how he was going to use it, and why it was important. The passion for his work emerged.

What had been a multiyear miscommunication became a tangible understanding. I helped him translate his ideas to a format his technology team could understand. Now, the technology team could design and build a solution. Just a few weeks later, the data began to give him new and essential information.

Soon afterward, I was headed down the hallway right when a board meeting was getting out. Greg shouted my name from the conference room door. This could either be a great thing or not. It went something like this:

"Douglas, wait!"

"Hi, Greg."

"The analysis is amazing. The board fully approved my idea!"

A little compassion, listening, and personal connection went a long way! Greg was able to show with clear metrics how his plan would improve both customer satisfaction and sales. His strategy got the green light. Plus, I got to hear some wonderful thanks for helping him.

COMPASSION

Compassion and creating a personal connection are not just feel-good concepts. They are good practices that yield results. When I brought compassion into my work with Greg, we solved his years-long analysis problem. That experience in the corporate setting reminds me of Jeanie Kortum-Stermer's work presented in the documentary film *Common Fire*.

Common Fire offers portraits of individuals who bring compassion and commitment to their work helping others. The film is coproduced by one of my doctoral professors Larry Daloz, who is also one of the film's researchers. He showed the film in one of his classes, and the story of Kortum-Stermer stays with me to this day. The homeless kids she worked with lived in transient housing because the shelters were full. While the kids received food and housing, she helped them with a deeper yearning. One she calls "the children's hunger for childhood." She further describes the hunger as an "emotional homelessness" where "they don't even live within themselves."[57,58]

It is monumental for those kids to know someone else knows they exist. She brings this knowing to them through the compassionate acts of focusing, listening, loving, and interacting. "It's extremely powerful when you put your hands around their face. And you say, 'Chris, you are such a good big brother, or Jasenya, that was a beautiful bouquet.' Whatever

---

57 Terry Strauss, "Common Fire: Leading Lives of Commitment in a Complex World," 1996.
58 Sharon Daloz Parks, Laurent A. Parks Daloz, Cheryl H. Keen, and James P. Keen, *Common Fire: Leading Lives of Commitment in a Complex World*, Boston, MA: Beacon Press, 1997.

it is, they're seen at that moment. They're seen, and in those moments, I think you kindle self."

While not as profoundly touched as the children in *Common Fire*, Greg's life and the tenor of his experience of frustration were similar. He had been pushed down for years trying to build innovative analytics with his own IT department incapable of making the leap to actually listen to him. Allowing him to be heard was all it took for me to bridge the communication gap. Truly seeing or listening to someone is a Forged leader's magic power.

Compassion is one of those terms that can mean something different to everyone.[59,60,61] Many people sense it as a kind of bonding with another person or feeling what they feel. Others see it as sharing another person's perspective. For Forged leaders, compassion emerges as an attention to the well-being of others and themselves.

You might get people to act more quickly by barking orders. This can be useful in emergencies. If one of your first actions is to assign a person to call 911, you must be clear who you're appointing. It's "You, call 911," not "Hey, could someone please call 911?" There's not much discussion.

---

59 Birgit Koopmann-Holm and Jeanne L. Tsai, "Focusing on the Negative: Cultural Differences in Expressions of Sympathy," *Journal of Personality and Social Psychology* 107, no. 6 (2014): 1092–115.

60 Tania Singer and Olga M. Klimecki, "Empathy and Compassion," *Current Biology* 24, no. 18 (2014).

61 Judith A. Halla, Rachel Schwartzb, and Fred Duonga. "How Do Laypeople Define Empathy." *The Journal of Social Psychology* 161, no. 1 (2021): 5–24.

But if order-barking is your primary, or only, form of motivation, you risk losing the connections made through compassionate interaction. This surfaces as a key challenge of Forged leaders. To develop working environments where people can feel supported to try new things, knowing sometimes they will fail as well as succeed.

Compassion offers safety for people to explore, experiment, innovate, and create. Without it, you'll be stuck acting under the rules of the old playbook, probably without even knowing it.

Note—Some of the Forged leaders interviewed for this book use the word *empathy* instead of *compassion*. Since the way they've used it is similar, I'll use the two terms interchangeably.

OUR BOSS JUST SHOUTS
One of my classes was assigned a room of beautiful and dignified wooden chairs, each bolted to the floor in perfect spacing. That layout represented what I would soon learn about some of my new students' work environments.

I asked the students for their experiences with daily standups. Daily standups are short (fifteen minutes) first-thing-in-the-morning get-togethers where team members give quick overviews of their project progress and challenges.

From the very center of the classroom, one student raised her hand.

"I hate daily standups," she told the class.

I asked if she'd share her experience.

"I hate them because our boss just shouts and threatens us, then makes impossible demands," she continued. "It's a terrible way to start every day."

She was right. That is a terrible way to start each day. I would hate it too. Anyone would. The purpose of holding daily meetings is to add transparency and support to people, not to threaten them. As more students raised their hand to echo her report, it became horribly clear this was a far too common transgression.

These kinds of daily dress downs are simply demotivating and debilitating. Who would want to risk trying anything new or creative in such an environment? In these situations, people tend to close down rather than open up. They move to the safe choice rather than the innovative choice.

I attended a talk once where the speaker told the global attendees (paraphrased): "We want to be more like Google. And we have to do it with one hundred percent success." This is the opposite of the Google mindset.[62,63] You can't strive for ultimate innovation and simultaneously be frozen by fear of imperfection. Forged stories teach us to foster new ways of thinking. You wield compassion and curiosity not borrow platitudes.

---

62 "Google X exec: We need to fail faster." CNN Business, Cable News Network, Updated July 26, 2021.

63 "Seven Lessons in Failing Forward from a Google Employee." Huffpost, HuffPost, Updated July 26, 2021.

THERE ARE BOUNDARIES

Let's say you're a team leader, and you decide to circulate and make personal connections with your staff. This could take place in an office or online. You might talk to Janet, whose daughter just made it to the honor roll, then Martin, who had a death in the family over the weekend, and so on through each team member. There are various ways of making meaningful connections with each individual every day, but beware, you can overdo it.

Nurses, for example, can experience *compassion fatigue* when working with trauma patients. They simply burn out by giving everything to their patients.[64] A study of 249 nurses who treated COVID-19 patients in intensive care and emergency rooms during the same year reported the following stress responses:[65]

- 61.0 percent reported insomnia
- 57.4 percent reported anxiety
- 39.0 percent reported depression
- 35.7 percent reported trauma
- 35.7 percent increased use of drugs or alcohol
- 27.3 percent received counseling

---

64 Vidette Todaro-Franceschi, *Compassion Fatigue and Burnout in Nursing: Enhancing Professional Quality of Life*, New York, NY: Springer Publishing Company, 2013.

65 Sasha Harry, "Predictors of Burnout for Frontline Nurses in the Covid-19 Pandemic: Well-Being, Satisfaction with Life, Social Support, Fear, Work Setting Factors, Psychological Impacts, and Self-Efficacy for Nursing Tasks." Doctor of Education Dissertation, Teachers College, Columbia University, 2021.

Once they reach the point of compassion fatigue, they are less able to give compassion to those they're caring for.[66] Without boundaries, you can quickly become depleted. So, as compassion-oriented leaders, you work toward creating space for others to build their well-being. You also nurture self-care to maintain healthy space for yourself.

While it might seem easy to dismiss compassion or even personal connection as a waste of time, Forged leader stories tell us the opposite. When Executive Producer Lotte Kronborg Thomsen leads massive animation projects for LEGO and the Paw Patrol TV series, her compassion surfaces in unpredictable situations.

THE SITUATION WAS DIRE

I received an introduction to Lotte Kronborg Thomsen through a mutual colleague in the arts who told me about her great leadership skills. When we scheduled our interview, I didn't know about the strong story of compassion I was about to hear. Lotte is now head of The Animation Workshop at VIA University College. She was living in London when we spoke during the pandemic.

She was also in London a few years earlier, working as Executive Producer on her next major animated project. Since the animation teams were remote, she stayed in the United Kingdom while the director flew to the remote location to

---

[66] Mareike Trauernichta, Elisa Oppermann, Uta Klusmannc, and Yvonne Anders. "Burnout Undermines Empathising: Do Induced Burnout Symptoms Impair Cognitive and Affective Empathy?" *Cognition and Emotion* 35, no. 1 (2021): 185–92.

work directly with the animation teams. Things were going well, but on a Monday night, Lotte received a painful phone call. The director, scheduled to return to the UK the next day, had tragically taken his own life in his hotel room the night before.

Lotte suddenly had to deal with families, embassies, and the logistics of transporting a deceased person home. But she still had to complete the project, now without a director. The situation was dire.

Lotte recalls, "There was no more money, they couldn't afford to be behind schedule, and the [remote teams] were suddenly left without creative leadership."

A DIFFICULT CONVERSATION
Lotte weaves transparency into her leadership style and brings people together by being open and creating a shared experience. So, she formed ways of communicating with the remote supervisors on a personal level while bringing the production to on-time completion.

Lotte found it complicated to help the supervisors understand they had to move forward without local creative leadership. She knew they had to feel safe in making their own decisions. Her instinct told her the only way was to be the person they could run their ideas by. So she arranged an online call with all of the remote supervisors to let them know.

How could she hold that difficult conversation? "In the remote location, culturally, you don't talk a lot about emotions, but you definitely don't talk a lot about when somebody takes their own life." While it would be challenging, Lotte prepared to speak with them. "And I felt I just needed to address it with the team because I needed to get them going."

WHATEVER YOU FEEL YOU NEED TO SAY

She had a call the next day with the supervisors to discuss the necessity for them to communicate with their teams from "the emotional side of it, and the mental side of it." Even though the project completion deadline was barreling down on the entire production effort, her first step was to help her teams find a way to speak about the tragedy. She ensured "people had a place to go to with however they would react to getting the news" and advanced the difficult conversation in steps.

First, she contextualized the situation. "I know we never talked about these things. And I know you feel really uncomfortable having to talk about these things."

Next, she broadened the conversation to both production and personal perspectives. "But we're on such a tight schedule," she told them. "If we don't talk about these things, it's going to impact our schedule. So, we're going to have to talk about it."

After building a foundation of support, she opened the discussion to allow the supervisors to talk openly. "Tell me if this really has affected you personally or if you feel uncomfortable," she told them.

Her next statement powerfully guided them directly into a discussion. "Whatever you feel, you need to say it now so we can actually deal with it professionally."

Her own conversation acted as an empowering example. "What I say to you now, go say the same to your teams."

Ultimately the animation team pulled together and created a highly successful result. A group that suddenly lost its director, and was not designed to work without creative supervision, successfully completed the project.

Even though the project completion deadline was barreling down on the entire production effort, her first step was to help her teams find a way to speak about the tragedy.

Lotte didn't bring the teams together through fear and threats. Instead, when faced with personal and professional strains, she brought compassion. She opened the discussion to the supervisors' own concerns and emotions. She also shared her own feelings while maintaining her boundaries by remaining a supporter, listener, and guide. Together, her actions released the teams to move forward under their own direction while staying available to support them.

The next Forged story portrays this as well, this time with Sunil Notani, the new leader on the block who had to find a way of bringing his colleagues together when the pressure was on.

TURNING IT AROUND

Sunil Notani is cofounder of the Transformation Group, a consulting firm specializing in enabling and leveraging digital transformations, and President of the New York Society for Information Management. He arrived in the United States fifteen years ago after successfully solving a major problem that brought FedEx to India. He required two items from his history of successful and strong leadership in his first major US position: trust and compassion.

Sunil's technology executive role quickly advanced to head of a massive product line. His not-so-small mission was to restructure a major international software company. But the company's organizational hierarchy was steep, and on his first global call, his new boss, a senior executive, aggressively challenged him and then abruptly ended the call.

Sunil quickly reached out to the other leaders on the call to apologize. He was concerned they were demotivated by the senior executive's antagonism. His compassionate outreach became their opportunity to get to know him. They returned the compassion in kind. "There was a lot of empathy from their side," Sunil noted. They felt how those aggressive conversations inhibited their own work, and now they saw how Sunil was championing them to change it.

TRANSFORMING AGGRESSIVENESS

Without missing a beat, Sunil seized the moment to increase the bonds through compassion. "Then I slowly worked with everyone, finding out what their issues [were, and kept] moving things forward until we got to an agreement." Through his care, listening, and personal connection, he enhanced the freedom for them to accomplish their goals.

Your team, staff, or organization picks up on your compassion.[67] New neural connections are created in the brain when compassion is learned.[68,69] These connections can be seen through functional magnetic resonance imaging (fMRIs).

You might experience compassion as a feeling or an "affective" encounter, but fMRIs make it clear neurological events occur in the brain as well. It is a physical manifestation.[70,71,72] Other studies show that compassion (toward yourself as well as

---

67 Brad Shuck, Meera Alagaraja, Jason Immekus, Denise Cumberland, and Maryanne Honeycutt-Elliott, "Does Compassion Matter in Leadership?: A Two-Stage Sequential Equal Status Mixed Method Exploratory Study of Compassionate Leader Behavior and Connections to Performance in Human Resource Development," *Human Resource Development* 30 (2019): 537–64.

68 Olga M. Klimecki, Susanne Leiberg, Claus Lamm, and Tania Singer, "Functional Neural Plasticity and Associated Changes in Positive Affect after Compassion Training," *Cerebral Cortex* 23, no. 7 (2013): 1552–61.

69 Olga M. Klimecki, Susanne Leiberg, Matthieu Ricard, and Tania Singer. "Differential Pattern of Functional Brain Plasticity after Compassion and Empathy Training," *Social Cognitive and Affective Neuroscience* 9, no. 6 (2014): 873–79.

70 Jean Decety and Kalina J. Michalska, "Neurodevelopmental Changes in the Circuits Underlying Empathy and Sympathy from Childhood to Adulthood," *Developmental Science* 13, no. 6 (2010): 886–99.

71 Maria Engström and Birgitta Söderfeldt. "Brain Activation During Compassion Meditation: A Case Study," *The Journal of Alternative and Complementary Medicine* 16, no. 5 (2010): 597–99.

72 Emiliana R. Simon-Thomas, Jakub Godzik, Elizabeth Castle, Olga Antonenko, Aurelie Ponz, Aleksander Kogan, and Dacher J. Keltner. "An fMRI Study of Caring Vs Self-Focus During Induced Compassion and Pride." *Social cognitive and affective neuroscience* 7, no. 6 (2012): 635–48.

others) can facilitate openness and engagement with others.[73] So, compassion is a two-way street. If you think your team will accept compassion in an environment where your heart is closed, think again. You need to get as good as you give.

TRUST AND TENACITY

Sunil began making calls straight after that initial meeting, and it took thirteen months to build the loyalty that led to his success. His compassionate approach also built a strong network of colleagues he could rely on. "Everybody knew me. My reputation was this guy gets things done."

When the pandemic hit, Sunil had just formed the Transformation Group partnership with a client base built through the same level of trust and support. And that trust goes a long way to move a client through the chaos toward their future state.

"So, imagine in today's environment," Sunil posits. "What happens when suddenly your entire business model is changed from underneath you? How do you react? How do you adapt?"

What happens is thoughts turn into decisions into actions with high velocity.

---

73   Shelia Wang, "A Conceptual Framework for Integrating Research Related to the Physiology of Compassion and the Wisdom of Buddhist Teachings," In *Compassion: Conceptualisations, Research, and Use in Psychotherapy*, edited by Paul Gilbert, New York, NY: Routledge, 2005.

Sunil applies those compassion skills even more so with a pandemic backdrop of staff witnessing friends and family losing their jobs. His words show how his compassion works at the level of transformation, "You know, what you thought was important is no longer important. You're suddenly moving to something else."

TEACHINGS AND LEARNINGS

Compassion is placed at the beginning of the Forged practices because it supports the entire model. Without compassion or the care for people's well-being and freedom—including your own—you cannot fully lead through volatile times.

To facilitate creativity and growth, you bring compassion with you into the Forge and get ready to build on its strength.

Think back on my students' stories, where getting browbeaten every morning was used as a motivational technique. Their leaders are not going to get useful results from that kind of fearmongering. The problem is even worse if you're working with a local or smaller team. In extraordinary moments, especially ones of decision and action, you want your team working in the compassion zone, not in the fear zone.

The bad news is there are leaders out there who are not sensitive to the use of compassion and personal connection during volatile times. The good news is many are, and they have wonderful stories to guide the rest of us.

CHAPTER 5

OWN THE UNEXPECTED

Coil hooks are industrial tools used to hold and lift everything from heavy wires to large shipping pallets. When they're properly cared for, they can secure high voltage cables to electrical towers in rural areas. In the summer of 2018, with seasonal Diablo winds gusting up to fifty miles per hour, a coil hook failed on one of the towers built about one hundred years earlier to bring power to Butte County, California. When the cable it was holding separated from its tower, it ignited the Camp Fire, one of the deadliest and most destructive California had ever seen.[74]

Less than two hours after the fire started, the nearby town of Paradise was in flames. Seventeen days later, eighty percent of Paradise had burned to the ground, and eighty-five people were dead. That most of the 27,000 residents of Paradise survived is due in large part to the brave firefighters who relentlessly battled the blaze.

---

74 CAL FIRE. "2018 Statistics and Events." https://www.fire.ca.gov/stats-events/. State of California: California Department of Forestry and Fire Protection, 2018.

WHEN WILDFIRE IS LIKE AN OCEAN

Firefighters work under continuously shifting situations. Uncontrollable factors like wind, terrain, and fuel keep them anticipating and strategizing their responses.[75] Park Williams, research professor in the Lamont-Doherty Earth Observatory, tells us, "The fire to me, it's like an ocean. It's so strong we don't really stand a chance of doing much to it."[76]

While there's not much you can do about the strength of the ocean, mindfulness instructor Jon Kabat-Zinn suggests, "You can learn to surf."[77] Once a fire ignites, firefighters have to surf through the ocean of extreme exhaustion and fatigue. They often move from one fire to another with little rest.

Jeff Carman, then District Chief of the Contra Costa Fire Protection District, shared his concern about his team. "With the intensity and ferocity of these fires right now, I'd be lying to you if I didn't say I worry about their safety while they're out there."[78]

Firefighters hear that concern when offered honestly. Job satisfaction for firefighters, people putting their lives on the

---

75 Andreas Bachmann, and Britta Allgöwer. "Uncertainty Propagation in Wildland Fire Behaviour Modelling," *International Journal of Geographical Information Science* 16, no. 2 (2002): 115–27.

76 Robinson Meyer, "The Simple Reason That Humans Can't Control Wildfires," *Science* 322, no. 4 (2018).

77 Kabat-Zinn, Jon, *Wherever You Go, There You Are: Mindfulness Meditation in Everyday Life*, New York, NY: Hyperion, January 1, 2021, p.ix.

78 Erin Ailworth, "California Firefighters Battle Exhaustion from Perpetual Blazes; Crews Go from One Wildfire to Another on Little Sleep; "I'd Be Lying to You If I Didn't Say I Worry About Their Safety," *Wall Street Journal (Online); New York, N.Y.* November 19, 2018.

front lines for others, increases when their leaders show care for and empower their teams.[79,80,81] Likewise, a study of 398 firefighters showed they engage in safer behaviors for themselves and fellow firefighters when they see their supervisors show an active commitment to safety.[82]

Like fire chiefs, Forged leaders hold the care of their team members paramount. They truly value and care about the well-being of their employees as well as the organization as a whole. As we'll see next, that work paid off when those concerns successfully drove the human resources response to pandemic upheaval in a large multinational corporation.

POSITION IT DIFFERENTLY

Spearheading Global Human Resources for a 114-year-old multinational company with 40,000 employees is a worthy challenge on any normal day. Toss in pandemic chaos, and it takes a superstar. Kathy Schreiner, Senior Vice President of Human Resources, Corporate Services for the Americas at Li & Fung, is that superstar. Kathy has been with Li & Fung

---

79 Kylie Bartolo and Brett Furlonger. "Leadership and Job Satisfaction among Aviation Fire Fighters in Australia," *Journal of Managerial Psychology* 15, no. 1 (2000): 97–93.

80 Summer Rachelle Felton Odom, "An Examination of the Preferences for Leadership Style of Firefighters of Different Rank and Generational Cohort" PhD, Texas A&M University, 2011.

81 "How Connector Managers Create Star Performers," Smarter with Gartner.

82 Todd D. Smith, Franklin Eldridge, and David M. DeJoy. "Safety-Specific Transformational and Passive Leadership Influences on Firefighter Safety Climate Perceptions and Safety Behavior Outcomes," *Safety Science* 86 (March 3, 2016): 92–97.

for over thirteen years, and the energy in her voice depicts her respect and joy in working for this family-run company.

The direct economic impact that volatile times had on Li & Fung's downstream retailers shifted buyers toward big-box retailers. These retailers also started selling face masks, and Li & Fung shifted to manufacture them. In the face of these changes, the old ways of performance management flew out the window, along with annual goal setting.

In response, Kathy created a conversational model of performance assessment aligned to team development. "What we are going to do is kind of position it differently because this is a different time. And we're going to say to the employees, here's a one pager, tell us what have you achieved this year. How has COVID affected you? Positive and negative both? What is it you want to see going forward in the future? What is it you see in the company happening?" These questions can work for the benefit of team members by giving them an understanding of how the company can help them perform their work.

Kathy's shift toward this new type of "assessment" encapsulates nearly all Forged leadership. This is especially evident when she opened the review process to hearing feedback from the employee. Imagine walking into your annual performance review, and your boss sitting across from you honestly asks, "What is it you need from us?" I have spent decades in consulting and full-time employment, and that question is a treasure when asked with sincerity.

The pandemic triggered Kathy's requirement for an unexpected worldwide shift in her organization. She successfully brought together diverse parties across geographically and organizationally disparate situations during a chaotic situation.

Kathy rewrote the playbook on assessment, solidifying her status as a Forged leader. She transformed a global organization in a way that reflects her values as well as the organization's. In the end, the new organizational model reflects her attention to the company's growth while simultaneously focusing on the well-being of its individuals.

Let's look at another case where high levels of expertise and creativity saved the day. This time in Sethretta Frank's story of saving her company and her team members' jobs.

NOBODY CAN TAKE THAT FROM YOU

Soon after Sethretta Frank began her new job as an engineer, she identified a disturbing problem. The segment of the company she joined was "up for grabs." They manufactured sputtering targets. Sputtering targets come up several times in Sethretta's story, so here's a simple way of understanding them. You take a material like gold and change it into something like ink. Then you paint that gold ink onto tiny electronic components that go into your phone, car, computer, TV, and refrigerator. You'll find them in almost every electronic device you own. We'll call them STs for short.

Why would a group that made them be threatened when they are used in so many devices? The problem was in the process that performed the magical change from gold to ink. It was decades old, and a lot of other companies performed the same magic. So Sethretta's company was just one more magician on the stage. It had reached what's often called the top of the S-curve.

As shown in Figure 5.1, the S-curve is a predictive indicator for life cycles across a variety of fields like nature or business.[83,84] At the bottom of the S-curve, you're an entrant into the field. Few others are doing what you're doing. There's more risk at the bottom of the S-curve, but it's the right position to hold if people want your product or service. For example, if you want to take a suborbital joyride, only a couple of vendors are approved by the Federal Aviation Administration (FAA) to take you there.

At the center of the S-curve, your product is a commodity, which means many others can provide the same product. If many vendors entered the consumer space race, the price for a flight would become more competitive.

At the top of the S-curve, the market becomes saturated. This is where your product, which was highly competitive when it entered at the bottom of the S-curve, is not competitive at all. If consumer spaceflight reaches this point, there will be so many competitive companies they will likely try to

---

83 Arthur M. Langer, *Analysis and Design of Next-Generation Software Architectures: 5G, IoT, Blockchain, and Quantum Computing*. Cham, Switzerland: Springer, 2020.

84 Theodore Modis, "Forecasting the Rise and Fall of Almost Anything." *The Futurist* 28, no. 5 (September-October 1994): 20–25.

reduce operational costs as their primary way of remaining competitive.

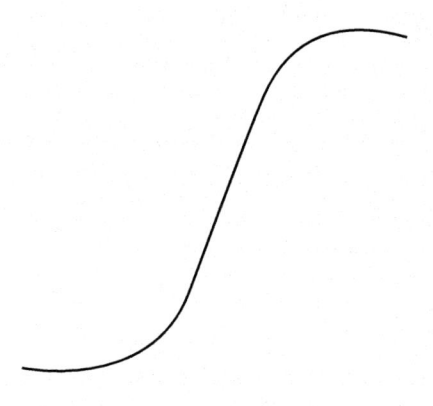

Figure 5.1: S-Curve Life Cycle

About six months after Sethretta started as an engineer at the ST company, she saw her new employer was at the top of the S-curve. STs were no longer a competitive product. The company was under threat of being taken over by another, and people's jobs were on the line.

"There was no new growth. Nothing was standing out," she told me.

There were few options for her. Stay with the company until the inevitable end or start another job search before her current employer was sold. But Sethretta came up with a new way no one had considered.

First, typical to companies at the top of the S-curve, she devised a streamlined process to create STs that reduced the time and cost of production. While that made the product less expensive to produce, it did not make it competitive. Sethretta questioned what would make buyers come to her firm above all the others that could make STs?

And the idea came to her: "I was like, huh, you know what? This is the manufacturing industry. Service is not something that they do. I think it would be so cool and so different to do STs as a service."

With that, Sethretta devised a completely new business-to-business service model that allowed other manufacturers to use her company's streamlined production model. Sethretta's company creates the product the way their client wants and uses any extra metal for other projects. If the client doesn't use some of the product, they can send it back to Sethretta's company for recycling into a different product. She had created a sustainable process.

The service model of manufacturing STs was so successful they did not sell the company, employees did not lose their jobs, and today that firm is the only one providing such a unique and competitive service. Sethretta brought them from the end of the S-curve cycle back to the competitive start.

•• ———— •◆• ———— ••

When the situation of her company being sold surfaced, Sethretta was motivated by values planted in her childhood and family life. She acted to protect the jobs of her colleagues. In owning that moment, she designed a unique and competitive solution. There is a repeating theme in her story leading to her motivation to save the firm. Whatever role she's handed, she brings her innovative sensibility to transform it to a new and improved role and the care of others.

When Sethretta's family moved to the United States from Sierra Leone, the entire family shared the one antenna TV in their efficiency apartment. Her mom supported the family by waitressing for $2.50 an hour.

Sethretta sums it up, "We didn't have anything."

But they did have a strong dedication to learning. Sethretta was brought to the US by her mother when she was just thirteen. "Just trying to get us to have a better education, a better life." She gives credit for her success to her upbringing. One way Sethretta remains connected to this moment in her journey is through her values.

"When you have certain values and morals that are placed in you, you kind of hold on to them."

The value of education remains stronger than loyalty to a specific job role.

"Jobs have no loyalty to you. None, zero. You can be making a gazillion dollars today. It doesn't mean they can't take that away. But your degree, nobody can take that from you."

And nothing would stand in her way.

Sethretta's education journey started strong. In high school, her teachers moved her into advanced placement classes. Later she was accepted into both local and more competitive colleges. But since she couldn't afford the more competitive colleges, she attended the local one.

Part way through her bachelor's degree, she took a ten-year hiatus from school to work and support her new family. The journey increased her deep values of family and grit. "Everything in me is coming from nothing to something. You know, nothing is too small, nothing is too big."

"When you have certain values and morals that are placed in you, you kind of hold on to them."

Those values guided how she interacted with her coworkers at the ST company. "I don't look down on anybody, no matter what title, no matter what grade. It doesn't matter because I treat everybody the same, regardless of their titles or position."

The ST company was about to reap the benefits of the hidden leader that snuck on board when they hired Sethretta as an engineer.

BUILD A GROUP CONSCIOUSNESS
Sethretta cared about her work and the people around her at the ST company. But she saw there was no community.

She set out to change that. "I started doing a birthday shout-out. I introduced having potlucks for the holidays." She even brought in new plants to replace the dead ones, literally bringing life to the office space. This was not in her job description. It was simply a continuous call to help others.

Sethretta's concern for her coworkers and environment became the primary impetus for solving the sputtering target firm's problem. It was necessary for Sethretta to help her coworkers, and necessity is the mother of innovation.

Greater employee engagement has been shown to increase profitability.[85] Sethretta's story is an excellent example. The values she grew up with guide her to this day. They show how genuine care for others above and below your hired role can develop and engage your community. Her idea to implement STs as a service was more readily accepted, since the organizational community was already engaged. At the end of the day, her company wasn't sold and the employees weren't laid off. Instead, they were honored.

TEACHINGS AND LEARNINGS
Whether in the form of a pandemic, the loss of a competitive advantage, or a wind gust that suddenly changes the direction of a wild fire, the unexpected happens.

Forged leaders own the unexpected and respond to it by saving lives, jobs, organizations, and homes. Owning the

---

[85] V. Kumar and Anita Pansari, "Measuring the Benefits of Employee Engagement," *MIT Sloan Management Review* 56, no. 4 (2015): 67–72.

unexpected is far more than making lemonade when given lemons. Forged leaders are driven by their values and choose their next actions accordingly.

For Kathy Schreiner, it surfaced as a new way to bring people from typically disparate areas of the Li & Fung corporation together, sustaining against pandemic-driven changes. The organizational changes Kathy made at Li & Fung were driven by her care for the company and its employees.

Sethretta Frank owned the unexpected when she learned her new employer was under threat of being purchased by another company. The company's core competency did not uniquely separate them from the other sputtering target manufacturers. Her concern for her coworkers brought out the leader in her, and an entirely new business model was born.

These Forged leader stories remind us that when unexpected situations occur, bringing care to the battle is not a sign of weakness. It is a core strength that drives innovation, change, and action.

CHAPTER 6

RECAST IDEAS

Mystic, Connecticut, is known for some fun activities. It's got that family-owned pizza parlor that starred in the movie *Mystic Pizza*, which introduced us to the up-and-coming Julia Roberts. Another attraction is the Mystic Aquarium, which boasts views of seals and turtles. My friend Jan loved to take her daughters there, stay overnight, and travel home the next day.

Usually, their trips back to New York were uneventful. One time, the traffic was relatively light on I-95 South in Connecticut, and it should have been a straightforward drive.

Without warning, a car painted in primer gray with a scrapyard finish passed them on the left and then moved directly in front of them from the fast lane. Jan sensed her calm trip was about to get dangerously more interesting. She kept a careful eye to the sides and behind just in case "Scrapyard" went out of control. It did.

Scrapyard drifted to the left, then too quickly corrected back to the right, and finally slammed its brakes, careening into an uncontrolled spin. The driver kept screeching the car into corrections that made it impossible to predict which lane it would cross in the next moment. Jan had just enough time to avoid Scrapyard, make a controlled slow down, and move to an opening on the left. Scrapyard was back in control, pulling over to the slow lane shoulder as Jan passed. This all happened in seconds.

It doesn't matter how much you train, prepare, or script solutions. Volatile times use your acute awareness of what's occurring in the present moment. You have to think and act in ways that are completely different than you've acted before. You have to innovate.[86]

Jan's normal drive home was suddenly and unpredictably different. Surprises like this take place in all kinds of situations. All indications might suggest you have a normal drive ahead, but that can change in an instant.

We tend to anticipate based on what's normal since we can only guess what might be the next new normal. We need to do better and prepare for the unknown.

In 1970 the crew of Apollo 13 could not have prepared for one of their oxygen tanks exploding 200,000 miles from earth. There were no backups for the oxygen tanks, but they had a set of NASA engineers whose job it was to think creatively. With no time to spare, the engineers designed a set

---

86 Douglas Scherer, "Using Reflective Learning in Information Technology Crisis Resolution," Chap. 9 In *The Dark Side of Technological Innovation*, edited by Bing Ran, 231–54. Charlotte, NC: Information Age Publishing, 2012.

of processes that used the onboard equipment to bring the astronauts home safely.

A key component in developing a creative sensibility that allows your team to respond like the NASA engineers is "contextual intelligence." It's a kind of situational awareness that speaks to your ability to understand what's happening in your environment and to respond with practical decisions.[87,88] Contextual intelligence asks that you look at something more insidious and often masked with unsurfaced assumptions that may be driving your action. In the end, it's a flight propelled by expertise, trust, and improvisation.

CHALLENGE YOUR HABITUAL RESPONSES
When you form a habit, you're hooked into a self-reinforcing cycle. You experience something that brings you pleasure (or at least something you want to happen again), which gets associated with an action. The link can form without you knowing it. For example, if every time you feel bad, someone gives you a treat to make you feel better, over time you can develop a habit that sees you reaching for treats every time you feel bad.

Habits can form without warning. In one study, individuals were trained that when a bell rang, they would be administered pain in the form of heat. The researchers found that eventually, they would ring the bell, and the people in the

---

87 Patrick T. Terenzini, "On the Nature of Institutional Research" Revisited: Plus ça Change...?" *Research in Higher Education* 54, no. 2 (2013): 137–48.

88 Richard K. Wagner, "Tacit Knowledge in Everyday Intelligent Behavior," *Journal of Personality and Social Psychology* 52, no. 6 (1987): 1236–47.

test would feel pain prior to the administration of heat. The pain reaction took control without them knowing it.[89]

Similarly, leaders who remain rooted in habit may react to challenges of leadership, even new, unexpected challenges, in the same way they did before, without really thinking about it. In contrast, Forged leaders respond based on what is happening in the present moment and challenge habitual responses while seeking more innovative ways to face the issue at hand.

Organizations, especially heavily hierarchical and siloed organizations, become reactive and inflexible in similar ways. They can even become victims of their own success. They perform well in an area, then feeling safe in that competitive space, they don't move beyond it. If an organization is not flexible and open to new and competitive product design, it may just repeat its old successes until they are no longer relevant.

Fear becomes a key contributor to this sequence. Since organizations tend to penalize failures, we lock into the things that saved us in previous situations even when the current situation is different. Conversely, Forged leaders who bring openness to their organizations can thrive when faced with new challenges. Openness sounds like a throwaway "soft skill," but we've seen how it can confront some of the biggest

---

89 Antoine Lutz, Daniel R. McFarlin, David M. Perlman, Tim V. Salomons, and Richard J. Davidson. "Altered Anterior Insula Activation During Anticipation and Experience of Painful Stimuli in Expert Meditators," *NeuroImage* 64 (2013): 538–46.

problems in leadership by motivating staff and the leaders to move beyond themselves.

You are better than you think.

The more you move away from preconceptions and organizationally imposed boundaries to creativity, the more you move toward improvisation. Improvisation takes everything you've practiced and brought to the stage and then lets you run wild based on the other actors, the audience, and your imagination.

Improvisation starts with expertise and then incorporates new circumstances and opportunities. Instead of arriving with a locked-in performance, you build something new. You dedicate yourself to the differences and know experiments don't always result in the expected. Live performances draw our attention to what's happening on stage. But leaders behind the stage make the performance run smoothly. If all goes well, you probably don't even know they're there. But when things get out of control in a live performance, they have to improvise rapidly. This is what happened to Peter Koletzke one night in Edinburgh.

WORK LIGHT

Peter is a highly sought consultant in Oracle application development. When I first met him, he was the Chair of the Database Application and Design certification program at Columbia University. It's a role he passed on to me when he moved to northern California in the dot com era. He also selected me as the contributing editor to one of his six books on Oracle software development, introducing me to the world of book writing. At that time, Peter traveled both for consulting and for his frequent appearances on the stages at Oracle technology conferences.

But before that, in the 1970s and 1980s, Peter was a stage manager and lighting designer for the Murray Louis Dance Company (MLDC). His work spanned everything from making sure the lighting was right to organizing the transportation of people and equipment and perhaps the more artistic work of lighting design. His design talents can be seen in YouTube clips of Murray Louis's piece, *Four Brubeck Pieces*.[90]

The artistic and caring vein constantly runs through him. I've sat with him in events ranging from Oracle database conferences to Paul Winter concerts in early mornings at the Cathedral of St. John the Divine, the largest cathedral in the world.[91] In both venues, Peter makes slight observances that heighten your experience. Like noticing how the sun rising in the east streams brilliantly through the purposely positioned stained glass windows of the Cathedral in coordination with the fourth hour of Winter Consort's early morning crescendo of a pipe organ, saxophone, chanting, and more.

Such observations seem small but gleam large. They're the kind of attention to detail that allows a dance company, on a different stage every few nights, to feel safe expressing themselves to audiences in different countries. That attention to

---

90 The City Center, NYC, "'Four Brubeck Pieces': Murray Louis Dance Company & the Dave Brubeck Quartet."

91 "About the Cathedral-Cathedral of Saint John the Divine," The Cathedral of Saint John the Divine, accessed July 17, 2021.

detail carries a large amount of responsibility. The result is part of the beauty of watching a live performance. The venue, the performers, the audience, especially if it's a traveling show, are all slightly different each evening.

When I listen to Peter's stories of being a stage manager to a touring company of dancers, I am really impressed. There is a high level of ingenuity, figuring out answers to unending incalculable problems, small and large, as they arise. But more than that, there is caring for the team, ownership, and responsibility for making sure their performing experience and the audience's reception to their performance are the best they can be. Each performance he sets the stage for the choreography, but it is yet fresh and in the moment to be experienced as unique each time.

For example, there was one particular performance at the Edinburgh Fringe Festival. The Fringe has run every year (except 2020) since 1947, from the beginning of August through the 25th. It originally began as an alternative to the Edinburgh International Festival, which grounds itself in classical music and dance traditions.

The Fringe Festival hosts all types of performers, and in 1982 they were hosting a hypnotist each evening before the MLDC took the stage. As is normal, nothing was normal. The layout was a Thrust stage, as shown in Figure 6.1, which has audience seating on three sides of the stage instead of in front. And the lighting design for the dancers was very different from that used by the hypnotist. This type of change requires quickly repositioning equipment and rewiring of electrical connections before and after each performance. What could go wrong?

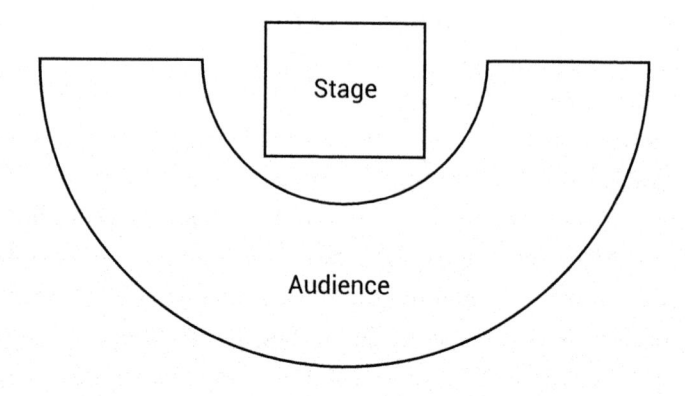

Figure 6.1: A Thrust Stage

One evening they found out. It was during a dance called *Index (to necessary neuroses)*, a piece representing the dark recesses of the mind. The stage is set, the soloist enters, Peter calls the lighting cue for a single spotlight focused on the soloist. And everything went perfectly. The effect was maintained, and the deep soul was portrayed... if only. Actually, that evening, when the setting changed from the hypnotist's show to the MLDC, one of the crew made a mistake in the wiring. Instead of the single spotlight illuminating only the soloist, a bright work light flooded the stage and audience. Not quite the designed effect. In fact, the soloist named this effect *Index on the Beach*.

Peter describes the scene, "...and the soloist just went on and did the thing, and we didn't stop the music or anything. We just figured out what had happened and said turn off that light, and they did. But meanwhile, there was a bit of a panic because it really kind of ruined the main effects for that piece. So that was a variation, kind of in the bad way how the piece was different that one night."

I don't think I've ever seen Peter in a panic. So, it's hard to imagine that scene in Edinburgh. It takes an open focus to take in the situation and work with the stage crew to trace the wiring in the middle of a performance. Especially when you've taken so much care, working with the crews, transporting performers and equipment, and creating a safe space for the artists to express themselves. But on this wild evening, which in ways represents every evening on the road, the unexpected mistake by a team outside his control was handled with a bit of quick response and a lot of calm and open focus.

Sometimes the unexpected happens to you, and sometimes you initiate it. Successful companies and leaders on the edge of innovative ideas and products all have this in common. They embrace the unknown.

Here again, they weave their improvisational skills, ideas that have never been thought of before, and ways of implementing them. In fact, they can sometimes fail at their attempts yet still learn something beneficial for the next experiment or performance. This occurs whether it's a stage manager, or as we'll see next, a concert pianist, or a member of the board of directors of a major airline advocating for superior internet access in the skies.

TRUE VARIATION

A couple of weeks before our interview, Virginia Gambale's name and photo were bellowed to Times Square and the world from the seven-story tall, ten-thousand-square-foot Nasdaq sign at the corner of 43rd and Broadway in Manhattan. Virginia had just been made a board member of Nutanix, a major cloud services provider, and has since become Chairwoman of the Board. She sits on five major public boards, including JetBlue—a major US domestic airline. Needless to say, Virginia is a powerhouse and a sought-after leader.

With the sun streaming from large glass windows behind her during our interview, sitting comfortably on her chair, her sense of ease in that space belied the position she occupies in her high-level leadership roles. Before entering the business realm, Virginia was a concert pianist. Whether in music or business, the balance of ease and professionalism can be a good starting point to see how expertise and awareness of your surroundings inspire you to flex your improvisational muscle.

There's enough of a difference between a live concert event and a recording to bring people to the theater. Part of the difference is the fandom thrill of seeing your favorite artist perform. It's also the energy of experiencing the music with a room full of folks who adore the artist like you do. But a large part is the excitement of what is happening live on the stage. Performances, while well-rehearsed, all have an element of the now: that performer, under that temperature and humidity, at that time with that audience. If you're a concert pianist, add one more crucial parameter—you don't bring your piano with you. You use what the venue provides.

IMPROVISATION ON STAGE

When Virginia walked on stage as a concert pianist, she played a rehearsed piece, but it was rarely on the same make or size instrument. Sometimes she was playing a nine-foot concert grand, other times a seven-foot semiconcert grand. No matter what type of piano she sat at while the audience savored her performance, it was a new situation at each concert.

As Virginia recounts, "So, you are in a lot of ways subject to a true variation. And, there are as many differences from one piano to the other as we have in people." But the unknowns of that moment don't end there. "Every instrument resonates in a certain way. The sound is different, and the keys are each constructed in a way where the touch might be harder or lighter or soft or uneven to a fault. Or the volume is not there. Or the treble is tinny, but the bass is rich. So, you never know what you're going to get."

You have to bring your expertise and practiced skills of adjusting to that specific situation, "and often you only get a few minutes before the show starts, as they say, to be able to perform on [that instrument]. So you at least know the variables in that situation through a little bit of experience because they are somewhat finite except for the acoustics of the hall, which is not always finite. And you have to really adjust on the spot."

Like many leader decisions, concert pianists have to work with a wide range of variables in highly visible situations. Rigidly sticking to exactly how you practiced a piece in the studio won't help when you have only moments to start the performance. Likewise, leaders who react through habit or from scripted responses will not get the job done. Adjusting on the spot, the ability to be flexible is crucial to leadership in volatile times. And it's a capability built by doing and doing again in other situations.

Not everyone can transfer their success and learning from one arena to another. But Virginia is a true Forged leader. She was able to leverage her experience on the stage as an asset in business.

"I think my training as a musician has made me very successful because of the ability to think abstractly on a consistent basis. And particularly in technology, learning technology is very abstract." When Virginia leverages these same skills in the boardroom, her command of the abstract and the ambiguous is a powerful combination. And without it, we'd probably be stuck on domestic flights without Wi-Fi.

IMPROVISATION IN THE BOARD ROOM
We pretty much take it for granted. You get on a flight, and you're able to connect to the onboard Wi-Fi. In fact, it is a major draw for many passengers. Inmarsat Aviation, a communications technology provider, surveyed customers about inflight Wi-Fi.

Eighty-one percent of parents traveling with kids said they would be more likely to rebook a flight on the same airline when it had Wi-Fi. The number rises to eighty-three percent when asking the same question to business travelers. But Wi-Fi quality tempers customer satisfaction. Fifty-four percent of those surveyed responded they would prefer not to have poor quality Wi-Fi at all.[92]

As a visionary strategic thinker, Virginia saw the need for great inflight Wi-Fi early on. Her strong ability to envision advancements is informed by practical grounding in life experience. She is a voracious reader, ingesting articles and staying on top of technological changes. But she does something extra. She sends the articles to others. She takes you along for the ride, informing you along the way and walking you through the justification of why she thinks things should change in a certain way. In short, she rapidly creates opportunities. As a great Forged leader, she is not resting on yesterday's successes. She instead is in a constant state of learning and transformation.

"And I brought that back to the team and the engineers, and I said, 'Guys, this is it, bringing Wi-Fi experience in the cockpit, as fast as you have at your home.'"

JetBlue was the first airline to bring live TV to seatbacks. They had Wi-Fi in the cockpit, but because it was slow, Virginia refused to allow it in the planes for passenger use. She was determined to bring great Wi-Fi to JetBlue, but building a better Wi-Fi experience is not that easy. It requires launching satellites and reconfiguring the planes. "And I brought that

---

92 Inmarsat Aviation, "Making Quality Count: Bring It On." *Global White Paper*, 2018.

back to the team and the engineers, and I said, 'Guys, this is it, bringing Wi-Fi experience in the cockpit, as fast as you have at your home.'"

At first, they met her vision with resistance. "They were like, 'What, Virginia? We fly airplanes. We don't launch satellites. We don't cut holes in our planes.'" I said, "Yes, but we can do all this, we can outsource the launching of the satellite, and we can get a partner to help fit the planes properly. We've reconstructed them for other things."

It took her two years. "I had to write numerous proposals, but we ended up doing it." Those fifty-four percent of travelers who would rather not have any Wi-Fi unless it's good have Virginia to thank for their great Wi-Fi experience. "Anytime I fly on a plane," Virginia told me, "and particularly on a Monday night, there are bankers and football lovers... just texting, back and forth, going from the East Coast to the West Coast. And I've heard bankers say, 'you know, I only fly JetBlue when I'm in the middle of a deal because it's the only Wi-Fi that's reliable and fast.'"

Bruce Lee's famous quote describes Virginia's power well: "When you pour water into a cup, it becomes the cup. When you pour water into a bottle, it becomes the bottle. When you pour water into a teapot, it becomes the teapot. Water can drip, and it can crash. Become like water, my friend."[93] How is her story like water? How is it flexible? She continuously learned, developing new ideas, and shared them with others.

---

93 Bruce Lee, "The Mandarin Superstar," By Pierre Berton. *The Pierre Berton Show*, September 12, 1971.

The qualities that make her a Forged leader carried her forward to success. She determined what the board needed to move the vision forward: some convincing, research, researching vendors, and multiple proposals. We hear a lot about grit. There was certainly grit in Virginia's persistence. But what tipped that grit toward success was her creativity and her improvisational way of listening and trying new ways of presenting her ideas and research to the other board members. Sometimes the way to pass through the Forge's heat is to be like water.

TEACHINGS AND LEARNINGS

Flexibility. Being like water. No matter in what situation they arise, Forged leaders meet them in the moment with the situation that's in front of them. Peter's and Virginia's stories reveal five qualities that support flexible thinking to work with volatile situations in creative ways.

QUALITIES OF FLEXIBILITY
- **Open Focus**
  - Open to new and dynamic ways of seeing things. Take a learning stance to the things around you and see the differences and perspectives.

- **Blending of Talents**
  - Find a balance between your expertise and your awareness of the situation. Use your open focus to find where your past experiences can be applied and where the moment requires innovation.

- **Improvisation**
    - Live performances are different than recordings. That's what makes it exciting and real. It also makes you think on your feet. Bring all your expertise and awareness of the moment, and then free yourself to act in ways you've never thought of before.

- **Abstract Thinking**
    - It all comes down to seeing things from a new perspective. While you're informed by your past experiences, volatile times force you to think in new ways, not be biased by your past successes or assumptions, and apply your knowledge to the present situation.

- **Persistence**
    - While you are acting, innovating, and improvising in the moment, that doesn't mean your effort will be over quickly. In some cases, you may be overcoming an emergency, like getting out of the way of an out-of-control driver, working with the idiosyncrasies of a piano, or dealing with a wrongly wired work light. But in other cases, the effort may take longer and require multiple iterations, like bringing Wi-Fi to an airline that isn't initially within its capabilities.

Finding your flexibility is sometimes easier said than done. Like most actions in your body, if you don't practice it, it atrophies. Flexible thinking challenges you to think and act in new ways. It's also one of the key ways of overcoming the success paradox. You don't always have to step too far outside your comfort zone. Sometimes you just have to get as close as a great Wi-Fi connection.

A good partner to flexible thinking is decision-making. One opens to new ideas, and the other helps rally around them. As we'll see in chapter seven, Forged leader lessons on decision-making emanate from the cockpit to the C-suite.

CHAPTER 7

GO WITH INTUITION

When I was young, my dad led an engineering team that designed power supplies for space missions. His team worked on the Surveyor project—the first vehicle to make a soft moon landing. When his company had a rare open house, I got to witness Surveyor through the large glass windows. It seemed gigantic. Years later, Apollo 11 was the first mission to land astronauts on the moon, using the best technology available—for 1969.

We were one of those households that tried to tune in to every launch and track mission progress every night. That July evening, we glued our eyes to the TV, but there was something we and most of the four hundred million other people watching across the globe missed. Mere hours before Commander (CDR) Neil Armstrong stepped off the ladder of the Lunar Excursion Module (LEM), a near tragedy occurred.

Four days and four hours into the mission, the LEM undocked from the command module and began its descent to the moon with Armstrong and Lunar Module Pilot (LMP)

Buzz Aldrin aboard.[94] About two hours later, they expected to begin their evaluation of the landing site. But what happened next was anything but standard. As shown in Figure 7.1, program alarm 1202 was triggered. The onboard computer overloaded.[95,96]

Day 5		CONFIDENTIAL	Page 175
04 06 38 22	LMP	Houston, you're looking at our DELTA-H. Program alarm.	
04 06 38 29	CDR	1202; 1202.	
04 06 38 40	CDR	What is it?	
04 06 38 42	LMP	That's in core ...	
04 06 38 46	CDR	Give us a reading on the 1202 program alarm.	

Figure 7.1: Snippet from the Apollo 11 command module transcript[97]

Armstrong, Aldrin, and Mission Control assessed whether they needed any changes in response to the alarm. Should they abort the mission, or could they continue the descent? Mission Control reviewed the alarm conditions and cleared the astronauts for landing. Turning their focus from the

---

94 National Aeronautics and Space Administration, *Apollo 11 Timeline*, National Aeronautics and Space Administration (Houston, TX: 1969).

95 *Apollo 11 Onboard Voice Transcription (U): Recorded on the Command Module Onboard Recorder Data Storage Equipment (DSE)*, National Aeronautics and Space Administration (NASA) (Houston, TX: June 21, 1969).

96 Mission Operations Branch: Flight Crew Support Division, *Apollo 11 Technical Crew Debriefing (U)*, National Aeronautics and Space Administration (Houston, TX: National Aeronautics and Space Administration, July 31, 1969).

97 97 National Aeronautics and Space Administration, *Apollo 11 Onboard Voice Transcription (U)*, 1969, p.175.

alarm, the astronauts discovered a new problem. The autopilot had finalized their landing site in a crater of rocks.

Armstrong looked through the Landing Point Designator (LPD), a set of scale markings on the window, and saw a good landing site in front of the crater. Would he be able to land there? "Continuing to monitor the LPD, it became obvious I could not stop short enough to find a safe landing area," Armstrong recalled in the technical debrief session.[98] He had to find an alternate landing site.

It was time to change the playbook.

With one minute of fuel remaining, Armstrong took manual control of the LEM. It was a split-second decision backed by situational awareness and years of experience. While he continued to sound calm, his heart rate jumped from seventy-seven to one hundred fifty beats per minute.[99] He picked a landing site beyond the crater, and with thirty seconds of fuel to spare, safely landed the LEM. Six hours later, his foot pressed onto the moon's surface.

Not all of us are called on to make first-time landings on the moon 240,000 miles away. But as we'll see, Forged leaders make highly impactful decisions during volatile times that draw on similar decision-making skills.

---

98 Mission Operations Branch: Flight Crew Support Division, Apollo 11 Technical Crew Debriefing (U), 1969.

99 Rachel Joy, "How Neil Armstrong Avoided Crash Landing on the Moon and Made History Instead," *Florida Today* (Viera, FL), July 18, 2019.

INTELLIGENT RISK AND INTUITION

In 2009, I interviewed C-suite leaders on how their life journeys influenced their leadership career paths. Jules, a C-suite executive at a Fortune 100 company, told me there are very few decisions made with one hundred percent certainty. "You cannot be in the technology business unless you take a risk. Now, you need to be intelligent about the risk, but you must take some risk."[100]

Every decision has some level of risk associated with it. When you choose a different breakfast cereal to purchase, you could wind up with a flavor you don't like. The influence of the decision is low, though. It's limited to one person and their taste buds. When you are an executive in a Fortune 100 company, the wrong decision could cost people their jobs.

Jules coined a great phrase to name the decision-making process in these situations, "Intelligent Risk." Intelligent risk takers use the best information they can get a hold of and balance it with their experience and values. Sometimes it works out like when she approved a ten-million-dollar project that netted five hundred million dollars. Still, getting to the point of making that kind of decision does not happen in a vacuum. It's learned. "Did I learn it all by myself? No, but I was fortunate to have people who could have that conversation with me."

Other decisions may not succeed, like when Jules implemented a streamlined process to reduce the completion

---

[100] Scherer, Levinson's Dream Theory and Its Relevance in an Academic Executive Mentoring Program, 2010, p.112.

time of a complicated set of tasks. It failed because the staff involved were not ready for the change. Jules always learns from these experiences as well as from the successes. "I looked at [the lessons learned] as forming basic principles around how I lived," Jules told me.

In other words, whether a decision succeeds or fails, Jules learns from it and incorporates the experience into her value system and into decisions the next time she takes an intelligent risk.

When Armstrong took manual control of the LEM, and when Jules followed intelligent risk, they both chose actions with some confidence of a positive outcome. But they weren't just relying on luck. They were relying on their values, skills, and expertise. Through applying experience and values, Forged leaders build these decision-making components into intuition.

There are many ways to understand intuition.

Forged leaders find intuition in moments that say, "I will never have all the information I need to make a decision in the time I have. But given what I know right now, I am making *this* decision and taking *this* action."

Going with intuition is not a random choice that succumbs to ambiguity. It might feel mystical because some of the information hides within your expertise and values. So, how do we unearth those elements?

Part of the answer comes to us from the Hotel Madison in 1938. This seaside location in Atlantic City, New Jersey, was home to the Kappa Delta Pi Convocation, a gathering of educational practitioners and theorists. Abraham Maslow, who designed the ubiquitous *Hierarchy of Needs* motivational theory, spoke to the Convocation in 1964.

But in 1938, educational philosopher John Dewey presented his lecture on a model of learning that emphasized "the organic connection between education and personal experience" as a path to determine action.[101] The lecture was later published as the book, *Experience and Education*.

UNEARTHING THE ELEMENTS OF INTUITION

Volumes have been written by and about Dewey. But his core philosophy is summed up well in this one sentence by Wilson and Hayes (2000). "As Dewey noted long ago... humans are agents in the creation of their own existence, not spectators."[102]

The freedom to make our own decisions stems in part from analyzing information and our reflection on its context. This includes questions like: How did we get the information? Who is requiring us to act? What biases or habits have entered our thinking? The answer boils down to the way our

---

101 John Dewey, *Experience and Education*, 20th ed. New York, NY: Macmillan Publishing, 1977, p.25.

102 Arthur L Wilson and Elisabeth R. Hayes, "On Thought and Action in Adult and Continuing Education," Chap. 2 In *Handbook of Adult and Continuing Education*, edited by Arthur L. Wilson and Elisabeth R. Hayes, 15–32, San Francisco, CA: Jossey-Bass, 2020.

beliefs, assumptions, and the meaning we give them color the information we use in decision-making.[103,104]

To make decisions, and especially intuitive decisions, we explore the meaning we give that information. Dewey's *Experience and Education* provides a model to understand that process called *the meaning of purpose*, which moves decision makers from observing a situation to taking action. In Forged leadership, learning forms decision-making and intuition. Plessner, et al. (2010) call this the *learning perspective*, which builds intuition from past experiences, context, and feedback.[105] Dewey highlights another key ingredient—meaning. Let's look at how that plays out to shape Forged leader intuition.

THE MEANING OF PURPOSE

While you might not always be fully aware of it, decision-making is a values-based proposition. Essentially, your decisions express what's important to you and even your internal purpose in life. As seen in Figure 7.2, Dewey identified five components that move you to action through a series of meaning assessments.

---

103 John Dewey, *Experience and Education*. New York, NY: The Macmillan Company, 1938.

104 Emre Soyer and Robin M. Hogarth, "Learning from Experience in Nonlinear Environments: Evidence from a Competition Scenario," *Cognitive Psychology* 81, (2015): 48–73.

105 Henning Plessner, Cornelia Betsch, and Tilmann Betsch. "Preface," In *Intuition in Judgment and Decision-Making*, edited by Henning Plessner, Cornelia Betsch and Tilmann Betsch. New York, NY: Taylor & Francis, 2010.

Based on his descriptions of each component, I have added a y-axis showing the level of interaction or focus each component has outside the self (external energy) versus focus on internal work (internal energy) like using expertise and reflection. The x-axis represents that the components generally flow from *observation* toward *intelligent activity*, but you may revisit the first four components in any order.

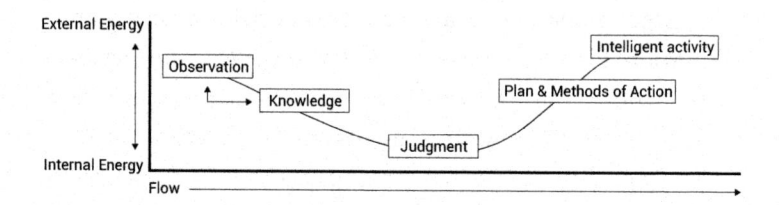

Figure 7.2: Dewey's Meaning of Purpose process

This is a process of self-reflection and liberation, of developing the freedom to think and act. In Dewey's words, "It is then, a sound instinct which identifies freedom with power to frame purposes and to execute or carry into effect purposes so framed."[106] In other words, we find freedom through exploring our purpose and then making decisions and acting on them.

It might help to think of the meaning of purpose as a board game in which you visit each one of the first four components (Observation, Knowledge, Judgment, and Plan) at least once to reach your decision and influence your actions. Your final decision increases in accuracy when you visit each component with honesty.

---

106 Dewey, Experience and Education, 1938, p.77.

That's all a bit heady. So, let's explore the meaning of purpose through the lens of Armstrong taking control of the LEM in the final moments before landing on the moon.

Observation
- In *Observation,* individuals try to objectively understand the circumstances and conditions of the problem.
  - Observation is close to External Energy because the person making the decision observes what's happening around them.

- LEM Example:
  - The autopilot finalizes the landing spot in a crater of rocks.
  - Rocky terrain, hundreds of thousands of miles from earth, radar going in and out.
  - One minute of fuel remains.
  - Program alert indicates the onboard computer is overloaded.

Knowledge
- *Knowledge* is an understanding of what has happened in similar situations in the past, gained from the individual's memory and the input of others.
  - Knowledge is placed close to the center of External and Internal Energy as it is the beginning of introspection and can be used as a guide in observation.
  - You need to be careful that previous knowledge does not turn into unchecked assumptions. For example, if you too often hear yourself saying, "Oh, I've seen

this before. I don't even have to think about it," your knowledge is probably holding you back. You want to considering thinking something more like, "Oh, this looks interesting. It's similar to the last time, but here are the ways it's different."

- LEM Example:
  - In addition to his training specifically for the Apollo 11 mission, Armstrong was a test pilot through the 1950s and 1960s, a period when NASA was losing about sixty-two pilots per week.[107] He brought that expertise to bear in the final moments of the LEM landing.

Judgment
- *Judgment* is an understanding of the significance of the individual's potential actions on the problem.
  - Judgment occurs through reflecting on observation and knowledge together with the intention of seeing what meaning they have for you and what your values and purpose are.
  - Judgment is placed closer to Internal Energy at the bottom of the diagram since it is an internal reflection process. How does this situation relate to my values? What does it mean to me and those around me? What are my assumptions and beliefs about this situation? What meaning does my purpose have for me?

---

107 James R. Hansen, *First Man: The Life of Neil A. Armstrong*. New York, NY: Simon & Schuster, 2005.

- LEM Example:
  - In the post-mission technical debrief, Armstrong clearly states what he values during the landing decision–safety and then science. "I initially felt that might be a good landing area if we could stop short of the crater because it would have more scientific value to be close to a large crater." Ultimately he chose a spot further from the research site in preference of his crew's safety.[108]

Plan and Methods of Action
- *Plan and Methods of Action* are created out of the individual's understanding of the previous components.
  - Here's where you bring together what you've learned through observing the situation and through internal examination to make a decision on what action you'll take. Your skills, expertise, and experience come together to form your final decision.
  - Plan and Methods of Action is higher than Judgment on the diagram (closer to External than Internal Energy) since developing your plan of action depends on interacting with the external world where the action will take place.
- LEM Example:
  - Armstrong intuitively reflects on the situation through observation, knowledge, and judgment and then chooses to land the LEM manually.

---

108 Mission Operations Branch: Flight Crew Support Division, Apollo 11 Technical Crew Debriefing (U), 1969.

Intelligent Activity
- *Intelligent Activity* occurs when you express through action what you've learned by way of the other four components.
  - Intelligent Activity is the external expression of yourself and the response you have chosen through reflection.

- LEM Example:
  - Having determined the plan and method of action, Armstrong takes control of the LEM with seconds to spare. "We then went into MANUAL and pitched the vehicle over to approximately zero pitch and continued."[109]

The meaning of purpose game asks you to be a bit vulnerable as you find out about yourself. The more practice you have, the clearer the process becomes. You don't have to be an astronaut to use this decision-making skill. As we'll see next, sometimes you just pilot a four-seater airplane.

WHEN THE QUESTION IS THE ANSWER

David Clarke is a successful engineer and entrepreneur. He is also a pilot. When he speaks about flying, his voice and eyes are energized and engaged. His openness to share his piloting experiences reveals his absolute joy of flying.

At thirty-five, he bought a Beechcraft A36 airplane. Twelve years before that, he started taking lessons and saving for

---

109 Ibid, p.9–24.

that plane. David remembers, "I always said, 'one day I will be able to afford a plane. I don't want to start learning then. I'll learn first and be ready when the opportunity arrives to own a plane.'"

> "If I'm asking myself this question, I already know the answer. I should go land. I can't hope my way past this."

And that strategy paid off. "You know, once I get that thing up in the air, it's like nothing else is in my mind." His joy of flying is instilled with respect for the art. He makes flight decisions based on safety. Like Jules's notion of intelligent risk that builds lessons learned into core principles, his experiences have developed into a series of life lessons.

There's a short distance between the blow an accident would have on those he loves and the decisions he makes for safety. "[An accident] would screw up a lot of people's lives. My children, my wife, my mother, my father, my sister, everyone who's ever known me." In spite of his joy in flight, he always errs on the side of intelligent risk. Especially when it helps avoid a forced landing.

Preparing to speak with him for this book reminded me that one of my most fun experiences was sitting in his copilot's seat. I'd only ridden in passenger jets, so this aircraft felt really small and close to the ground. When that thing took off, I felt the woosh of liftoff and knew firsthand where David gets his enthusiasm.

When you copilot with David, you get to wear the cool headset allowing you to talk to the pilot over the engine noise and help perform pretakeoff and landing checks. One of the things I learned that day is the importance of trusting yourself over your gauges. He showed me how to manually check the fuel level. He cautioned if you don't check the tank yourself, and your tank is low, it's your own fault if you run out of fuel, even if the gauge shows the tank is full. This value of responsibility and self-trust is one of his decision-making lessons.

One time David was flying home from a multistop round-robin between Portland, Maine, and Teterboro, New Jersey. He had been doing normal fuel consumption calculations since the plane he was in did not have a fuel totalizer computer. A fuel totalizer computer calculates various parameters such as real-time mileage and distance-to-empty information. Then the fuel question came up.

"As we were approaching Bridgeport, Connecticut, the thought went through my mind. 'I wonder if I should stop and fuel up? I don't think I need to. But I am calling it close.'"

This is the intuitive voice of experience. The question entered his mind, and it guided his action. "And I'm like, if I'm asking myself this question, I already know the answer. I should go land. I can't hope my way past this."

"So, I stopped, added forty minutes to the trip. After the plane was refueled, I looked at the total gallons that were pumped back into the plane. It was four gallons more than I thought there should be." David had made the correct decision based on intuition. If he hadn't stopped to refuel, even though he'd made very careful fuel calculations, he would have run out of fuel over the Bronx.

SCRAMBLING FOR RESOURCES

Safety decisions in the air might not seem to relate in any way to choosing a data center. But Eric Yuan, President and CEO of Zoom, experienced decision-making conditions in the five months between December 2019 and May 2020, which saw an increase by 6,000 percent in the number of daily Zoom meetings. "We did not design the product with the foresight that, in a matter of weeks, every person in the world would suddenly be working, studying, and socializing from home," Yuan told *Business Insider*.[110] As Zoom usage exploded, the Zoom servers maxed their capacities, and security breaches started making headlines.

The company scrambled to find additional server resources, which they did, in China. This location caused a backlash from corporate and government realms—even from members of the US Congress who then called Zoom a "Chinese entity we've been told not even to trust the security of."[111,112]

---

[110] "Meet Eric Yuan, the Founder and CEO of Zoom, Who Has Made over $12 Billion since March and Now Ranks among the 400 Richest People in America," Insider, Updated July 31, 2021.

[111] "Nancy Pelosi called Zoom 'a Chinese entity,' but it's an American company with an American CEO.," CNBC.com, Updated August 21, 2021.

[112] "Meet Eric Yuan, the Founder and CEO of Zoom, Who Has Made over $12 Billion since March and Now Ranks among the 400 Richest People in America, Insider, 2021.

Zoom realized their error and moved the additional capacity out of China. But Yuan had to reply to the backlash and rebuild confidence in Zoom's enhanced security features. Yuan's intuition brought him back to his values, and his response harkened to what his dad had taught him as a child, "hard work and stay humble."[113]

Yuan apologized in multiple venues, recognizing "we have fallen short of the community's—and our own—privacy and security expectations. For that, I am deeply sorry, and I want to share what we are doing about it."[114] That sentiment is echoed in Yuan's description of Zoom's corporate culture, "deliver happiness."[115]

TEACHINGS AND LEARNINGS

Forged leaders make decisions guided by information, values, and expertise. Now let's look at Table 7.1 and see how David's and Eric's decisions might map to the two models of decision-making described in this chapter: Dewey's meaning of purpose and Jules's intelligent risk.

---

113 "Eric Yuan, a Tech Boss Riding a Geopolitical Storm," FT.com, Financial Times, Updated July 9, 2020.

114 "Meet Eric Yuan, the Founder and CEO of Zoom, Who Has Made over $12 Billion since March and Now Ranks among the 400 Richest People in America, Insider, 2021.

115 Yuan, Eric. "Zoom CEO Eric S. Yuan: How to Manage Customer Experience?" *CxOTalk*. Cambridge Publications. May 28, 2021.

Table 7.1

Meaning of Purpose Component	Intelligent Risk Aspect	David Clarke—Stopping for Fuel	Eric Yuan—Relocating Servers
Observation	Information, knowing what's really happening right now.	Flying over Bridgeport, CT airport, raising a question about his fuel level	Servers have reached maximum capacity, and placement of new servers in China has caused backlash
Knowledge	Lessons learned through experience	Gauges can be wrong. Asking the question = the answer to the question	Zoom has fallen short of its own, and its community's expectations of privacy and security
Judgment	Values, Purpose, Meaning. Why am I doing this—what drives me?	His concern for those he loves and cares for far outweighs a potential forty-minute delay	Eric is guided by his father's teachings of hard work and stay humble
Plan and Methods of Action	Skills, Experience, Expertise	Landing the plane at Bridgeport will allow him to check and refuel	Next steps are to move the servers out of China and apologize to the public
Intelligent Activity	Taking Action	Saving lives by landing the plane at Bridgeport to add fuel	Servers are moved, public continues to use Zoom

Table 7.1: Examples of The Meaning of Purpose and Intelligent Risk Decision-Making

David's and Eric's scenarios teach us that you can build decisions using information about the situation, values, and expertise. Based on those decisions, you can take specific actions in the public sphere, which can become an outward expression of your values.

NOW IT'S YOUR TURN

Think of a decision you recently made or one you are making right now, where there are uncertainties and pressures. Add your story details below in Table 7.2, which I call *The Forged Leader Intuinator*. This is a chart to assist you in building your intuitive decision-making skills.

INSTRUCTIONS

- In the shaded top row, add your name and provide a story title to your decision.
- In the row labeled Observation, write down what you know about the situation, who it affects, and in what ways.
- In the next row, Knowledge, add what your experience tells you about this situation. Remember that knowledge and observation inform each other. What does your experience tell you about what you've observed?
- Next, use the Judgment row to record what values come into play and apply them to the situation.
- Based on your previous responses, consider your Plan and Methods of Action. Since this is a new situation with no proven solution, you may find a solution you hadn't thought of before.
- In a real-world scenario, this would be the time to execute the plan or Intelligent Activity, given your acceptable level and assessment of risk.
- Revisit the title of your story in the shaded first row. Does the story still correspond to what you learned through the intuinator? If not, update it now with a better story title.

Table 7.2

Meaning of Purpose Component	Intelligent Risk Aspect	Your Name—Your Story Title
Observation	Information	
Knowledge	Experience	
Judgment	Values	
Plan and Methods of Action	Expertise	
Intelligent Activity	Taking Action	

Table 7.2: The Forged Leader Intuinator

Now that you've investigated your individual stories of decision-making let's look at how collaboration and community help you in the new playbook.

CHAPTER 8

EMPLOY ACTION COMMUNICATIONS

Trees hid the corporate headquarters from the narrow, winding road that led to the top of the hill. The road opened to a large parking lot and office building. I was there to interview another C-suite executive for my research on leadership mentoring. After being led to her office, without delay, she showed me a piece of paper with a few sentences on it.

Her company had bought another, and she was handed a huge portion of the acquisition responsibility. The piece of paper contained her entire instructions. I'm paraphrasing, but it essentially said, "We are merging with company X. Please complete the integration." High impact and low information—this one's easily identifiable as a volatile time, one that's rife with change and ambiguity.

When required, Forged leaders beat paths where there were none or redesign old paths for updated needs. They understand that changing a business or an organization radically unsettles almost everyone involved. So, at times of transformation, they build paths of communication.

MAKING THE PATH

It's easy to visualize walking paths, so we'll start there. Some paths are designed into grids that appear more orderly but may not be the walkers' preferred route. Other times path designs develop through daily patterns of use. These are often called *desire lines* or *desire paths* since they indicate where the walkers want to go and how they feel most natural getting there.[116,117]

Numerous university campuses, for example, are crisscrossed by paths that were designed unknowingly by the people walking from one place to another. As students, teachers, and staff walked between activities over unpaved areas they tramped trails into the ground. Vegetation got packed into brown dirt and frayed grass.[118,119,120]

To illustrate, the path in Figure 8.1 is similar to the one in front of Grainger Hall at the University Wisconsin-Madison.

---

116 Lesley Malone, *Desire Lines a Guide to Community Participation in Designing Places*. London, England: RIBA Publishing, 2018.

117 "Desire Line," Merriam-Webster.com dictionary, Updated September 6, 2021.

118 "Maryland Images Tour Guides Share What You Might Not Know About the University of Maryland," ULoop, University of Maryland, 2012.

119 "The Road More Traveled: When to Take or Change the Paths of Least Resistance," Matthaei Botanical Gardens and Nichols Arboretum, Updated June 20, 2017, accessed September 5 2021.

120 "'Desired Paths' May Be the Key to Sidewalks at Some Universities," NBC 9 News, 2018.

To save time, walkers made a shortcut through the trees between West Johnson Street and North Park Street.[121]

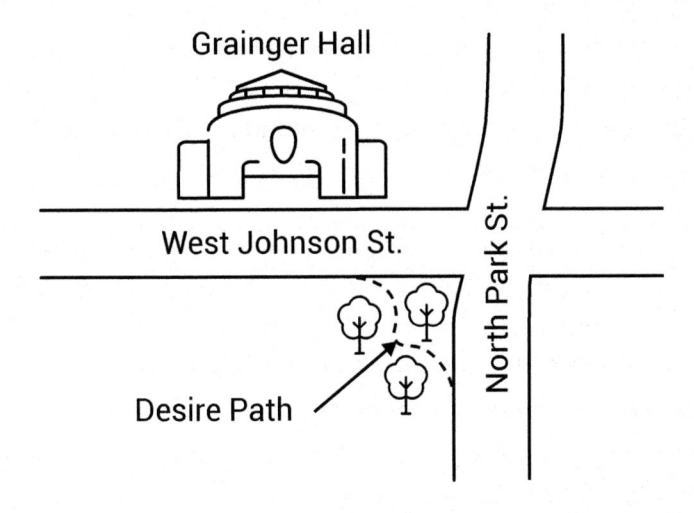

Figure 8.1: A desire line in front of University of Wisconsin Grainger Hall

Desire lines tell us something powerful about paths. They are at the same time the vehicle of communication and the message itself. Our steps express our intentions.

The same is true for the actions we take. The way we interact with others communicates our intent and values. It is what I call *Action Communications*. I've based the idea for the term Action Communications in part, on the Yorks, et al. 1999 definition of *Action Learning*: Action Learning is "an

---

121 "Desire paths: the unofficial footpaths that frustrate, captivate campus planners," W News, University of Wisconson-Madison, Updated September 6, 2021.

approach to working with and developing people that uses work on an actual project or problem as the way to learn."[122] Just substitute the word "communicate" for "learn" in their definition, and it works well to describe how action is communication revealed in the work we do for and with others.

In volatile times Action Communications are significant for two key reasons.

- **Transformation or Stagnation** Companies that don't continually adapt and change will likely not move forward
- **Accelerated Communication** Technology has increased the speed of communication

Let's look at each.

TRANSFORMATION OR STAGNATION

Companies that don't continually reflect and transform will potentially fall so far behind that they can't keep up. Donald Schön was a thought leader in organizational development. His writings on "the stable state," or infinitely doing things the same way, seem particularly appropriate for volatile times. "Constructive responses to the loss of the stable state must confront the phenomenon directly. They must do so at the level of the institution and of the person."[123] Schön's "stable

---

122 Lyle Yorks, Judy O'Neil, and Victoria J. Marsick. "Action Learning: Theoretical Bases and Varieties of Practice," *Advances in Developing Human Resources* 1, no. 2 (1999): 1–18, p.3.

123 Donald Schön, *Beyond the Stable State*. New York: Random House, 1971, p.29.

state" is one in which organizations are stagnant, often en route to a complete stall.

In Schön's writing, institutions must continuously learn and change themselves to bring about "their own continuing transformation."[124] Communications were slower then, but the message of continued transformation was just as clear. The dynamic nature of volatile times compels transformations. As leaders, Schön states, "We must learn to understand, guide, influence, and manage these transformations."[125]

When applied to organizations, Schön's learning process creates a bit of an infinite spiral where transformation occurs based on the continuous influence of leadership, organization, individuals, and technologies. For the influences to work, the organization must have a strong foundation in communication. As we're about to see, something special happens when Forged leaders communicate. They make it personal.

More than building paths for communication, Forged leaders create initiatives based on their values. They understand transforming an organization takes commitment to both the purpose and the people. Most importantly, Forged leaders show their commitment through the things they do.

There is a poem published in 1912 by the Spanish Poet Antonio Machado that describes that commitment beautifully.

---

124 Schön, Beyond the Stable State, 1971, p.30.
125 Ibid.

EMPLOY ACTION COMMUNICATIONS · 145

Traveler, your footprints are the path and nothing else; traveler, there is no path, the path is made by walking. The path is made by walking, and when one looks back one sees the path that one will never tread upon again. Traveler, there is no path, Only wakes on the sea. Translation by Nélida Quintero (2021)	Caminante, son tus huellas el camino, y nada más; caminante, no hay camino, se hace camino al andar. Al andar se hace camino, y al volver la vista atrás se ve la senda que nunca se ha de volver a pisar. Caminante, no hay camino, sino estelas en la mar Antonio Machado (1912)[126]

Forged leaders *make the road by walking* in two key ways:

- They imbue their team members with the power to investigate, learn, grow, and bring fresh ideas back to the group.
- They communicate through their actions as well as their words. Communicating their thoughts, they decide, and they act.

ACCELERATED COMMUNICATION

Advances in technology have increased the necessity to bring a focus to communication. Table 8.1, for example, shows how dramatically the speed of communication has increased since the age of broadcast radio. Table 8.2 presents an analysis discussed in Schön's book to show a similarly accelerating trend of integrating technology into broad populations. The bottom line is, things are getting faster.

---

[126] Antonio Machado, *Poesías Completas De Antonio Machado*. Madrid, Spain: Publicaciones de la Residencia de Estudiantes, 1917, p.229.

Medium	Time to reach Fifty Million Consumers
Radio	38 years
Internet	4 years
Twitter	9 months
Pokemon GO	19 days

Table 8.1: Modified from Langer's Time It Took to Reach Fifty Million Consumers.[127]

Invention	Time Required for Diffusion in Years
Steam Engine	150–200
Automobile	40–50
Vacuum Tube	25–30
Transistor	About 15

Table 8.2: Modified from Schön's Time for Technological Innovations to Spread Broadly Throughout Populations of Users.[128]

As fast as communications media have advanced, the speed it takes for messages to move digitally through an organization is even faster. In most organizations, messages move at the swiftness of instant messaging, or at worst, at the rate of a phone call.

Reaching so many users so quickly comes with a punch. Nintendo's second-quarter earnings report of 2016 shows they made 115 million dollars from Pokemon GO licensing fees.[129,130] In 2018 Pokemon GO made an estimated 795 mil-

---

127 Langer, *Analysis and Design of Next-Generation Software Architectures*, 2020, p.7.
128 Schön, Beyond the Stable State, 1971, p.24.
129 Nintendo Co, LTD., *Consolidate Financial Highlights*, Nintendo (Minami-ku, Kyoto: October 26, 2016.
130 "We Finally Know How Much Nintendo Made from Pokémon Go." Quartz, Updated July 1, 2021.

lion dollars worldwide.[131] By the end of 2020, Pokemon GO had a lifetime revenue of over 4 billion dollars.[132]

Communications internal to your organization are just as powerful. A 2010 study found hospitals in the United States lose 12 billion dollars annually due to poor internal communications.[133] While effectual communication can avoid financial loss, it can also boost the bottom line. A Watson Wyatt 2004 survey of 267 US organizations showed an increase in market value of 29.5 percent associated with effective internal communications, as reported by the Institute for Public Relations.[134]

It's clear. A lot is at stake from external and internal communications. Columbia University leveraged that knowledge when they chose a seasoned communications expert for their Executive Vice President for Public Affairs.

ACTION SPEAKS

When Shailagh Murray joined Columbia University in 2018, her welcome note to the school represented her humble style.

---

131 Stefanie Fogel, "'Pokémon Go' Global Revenue Grew Thirty-Seven Percent in 2018 (Analyst)," *Variety* January 3, 2019.

132 "Pokémon Go Hits $1 Billion in 2020 as Lifetime Revenue Surpasses $4 Billion," Sensor Tower Blog, Sensor Tower, Updated July 1, 2021.

133 Ritu Agarwal, Daniel Z. Sands, Jorge Díaz Schneider, and Detlev H. Smaltz. "Quantifying the Economic Impact of Communication Inefficiencies in US Hospitals," *Journal of Healthcare Management* 55, no. 4 (2010): 265–81.

134 "Connecting Organizational Communication to Financial Performance—2003/2004 Communication ROI Study," Institute for Public Relations, Updated August 1, 2021.

"Warm greetings from your newest neighbor," it opens. "I'm not the most obvious person to step into this role."[135] Yet, her background is illustrious.

Columbia University's President Lee Bollinger summarizes her background like this: "Clearly, Shailagh's exceptional depth of experience—at the highest levels of journalism and government and as a trusted advisor both to Vice President Biden and to President Obama on a wide range of policies, communications, and legislative issues—makes her extraordinarily well-suited to this position and to serving the current and future needs and interests of the University."[136]

Shailagh brought communication skills she forged by designing what was then a new strategy of using the internet and social media to advance political branding. "I won't even call it a process strategy," Shailagh recalls. "Because we just took all the digital opportunities and converted them into this bigger, more modern, more multidimensional media strategy or communication strategy." Fans of the TV show *Parks and Recreation* might recognize her handiwork in booking Biden for two appearances on that show.

Three years later, her initiatives, actions, and results corroborated Bollinger's prescient statement. She leveraged her passion for community building and her deep experience in political communication to heighten the Columbia University message internally to the university and externally to

---

135 Shailagh Murray, "A Letter from Executive Vice President Shailagh Murray to the Community," *Columbia University*, December 12, 2018.

136 Lee C. Bollinger, "Shailagh Murray Appointed Executive Vice President for Public Affairs," *Columbia University*, September 05, 2018.

the surrounding community. It's hard to share only one of her stories so let's focus on two that show how she built the expertise of her internal team and then engaged the external community through action communications.

BUILDING INTERNAL EXPERTISE

The evening before I interviewed Shailagh, I was teaching my master's students about change agents through the writings of Edgar Schein, a well-known researcher, and theorist in organization psychology and leadership. The way he describes the work of change agents might have been written specifically for the way Shailagh developed her staff. Schein's change agents stimulate *cognitive redefinition* or seeing their work in new ways, so they want to learn.

In Schein's description, change agents don't tell their direct reports how to do their work since that would limit their creativity and learning. Instead, they create an environment for them to seek new perspectives on solving problems.[137]

Upon arriving at Columbia, Shailagh knew straight away she had to boost the skills of the University's communications team. The video team, for example, had great skills and potential. "We had a great video team, but they were making seven- or eight-minute-long videos." Now, visitors only stay on the site for a few minutes. The change agent in Shailagh kicked in, and she set out to create a team of learners and

---

137 Edgar H. Schein, "The Role of the CEO in the Management of Change: The Case of Information Technology," In *Information Technology and the Corporatation of the 1990s*, edited by Thomas J. Allen and Schott Morton Michaels, New York, NY: Oxford University Press, 1994.

thinkers. Instead of telling the team what to do, she set an environment for them to discover ways of improving.

In that way, Shailagh's story reveals a genuine change agent. "So, I wasn't going to tell them. I needed to show them the marketplace was different and it kind of evolved since they had locked into this model three or four years ago. I wanted them to figure out on their own that a two-minute video is better," Shailagh recalls. "To me, that's really the definition of a successful organization, one that's confident and strong enough to have different perspectives embedded in the process from the bottom to the top."

Where does this Forged leader begin transforming her team? At the place of most immediate effect. "I think the key is to identify some kind of low-hanging fruit type opportunities, and show people as quickly as you can, the outcomes they can expect if they change their approach or think about things differently," Murray said.

Schein concludes that this form of transformation is one that sticks. "For the change to last, the target not only must learn new behaviors but also must cognitively redefine the issue, so new perceptions, attitudes, and feelings are created as well."

READYING FOR CHANGE
You might not be able to predict the future, but you can at least tell when your team is working in the past. Forged leaders don't just react to volatile times. They create an environment that encourages opportunities to transform as preparation for when the fire strikes next.

Shailagh created the environment for her team to change through exploration. That prepared them for something they would never know was coming—the COVID-19 pandemic. "We scrambled to launch this special site where we would put all of the COVID-related information on it." Its use soared. Columbia website metrics increased from about eight thousand visitors per day to about thirty thousand. While the campus was shutting down, Shailagh's team leveraged their transformation to support multiple communities in that defining volatile moment by initiating their COVID website.

You might not be able to predict the future, but you can at least tell when your team is working in the past.

Of course, Shailagh exudes pride in her team, "That same team, that same 1970s style team is now this team that's producing that [COVID website]."

Since Shailagh is a community builder, creating an effective website was only the beginning. From there, it progressed to direct benefits and interactions with the community. "When COVID started, and we started to do this series of town halls, we saw this as a great opportunity to connect, to establish a much more meaningful relationship with the neighborhoods because we can actually help them do something. So we held this series of seven or eight town halls on all these different subjects. And we started this emergency loan fund out of my office, that is now run by the business school and controller, to help local businesses."

Seeing how Shailagh wields her expertise and empathy through her communication skills, it may be time to update communication theorist Marshall McLuhan's saying "the medium is the message" to "your actions and intentions are the message."[138]

TEACHINGS AND LEARNINGS

The stories Shailagh shared all carried common themes of community values expressed through action and taught us that Forged leaders are action communicators. The characteristics of Action Communicators can then be summed in four core qualities:

- You afford humility.
  - Forged leaders tend to have humble assessments of themselves. Shailagh Murray sees herself as perhaps not the most obvious person to step into the role of Executive Vice President for Public Affairs, but in fact, her expertise, leadership, career—and results—show how impactful her work is to the community.
  - Humility does not mean you undersell yourself—it means:
    - You are aware of how you integrate with and support others.
    - You keep an open mindset. You play with letting go of your ego and appreciate that you might not know absolutely everything. The end product is

---

[138] Marshall McLuhan, *Understanding Media: The Extensions of Man*. CreateSpace Independent Publishing Platform, 2016.

not only the formation of new perspectives for you and your group, but also team members who feel part of the creative process.

- You create an environment for your team to change by supporting cognitive redefinition.
  - You engage them in ways that offer challenges and responsibility while supporting their search for new perspectives on ways of doing things differently.
  - You don't freeze the new perspective as to how you will do things forevermore. You do not rest on the laurels of the new normal.
  - You allow yourself, your staff, and your clients to continually reassess and learn, creating an ongoing learning environment that prepares for the next volatile time rather than operating as if in the past
  - In short, you allow your team to be innovative.
- You communicate through actions. You make the road by walking it.
  - You recognize your purpose and intent, and then you take actions
  - You realize the output of action communications is the de facto creation of community. Your own leadership, values, intent, and actions guide those same qualities in the community you build.
- You act first where you can make the most immediate effect.

Actions speak louder than words, even small actions. We've seen in this chapter how action communications and team transformation directly impact communities. But how do individual Forged leaders establish and sustain communities? *Hint for chapter 9—The seed of small communities has real lessons for mature trees.*

CHAPTER 9

DRIVE COMMUNITY BONDS

"You know, I've never watched one of the *Survivor* shows, but it's absolutely the opposite of how you survive. It's about the last guy on the island. If you're the last guy on the island, you're dead. The way to do it is, how do you be on the island with a bunch of folks so you can help each other? That's the world that we live in. And that's the way human beings have survived."[139] When Tom Chapin told me this in an interview for my sustainable leadership podcast, the message was clear. We are here for each other.

Tom is a Grammy award-winning master storyteller and musician who continues the folk music legacy of the Weavers and many others. I intended to interview him for just fifteen minutes and focus the conversation on his transition into the board of the philanthropic organization World Hunger Year

---

139 Tom Chapin, "Talk About Things That Matter." By Douglas Scherer, Voices of the Cliff, no. 6. Douglas Scherer. March 29, 2011.

(WHY). We wound up talking for a full hour and covering a wide range of issues ranging from the importance of art in schools to the essentials of making communities work.

"What again moves me," Tom said, "is how can we move this whole thing in a positive direction? How can we make it so that this is a world that can sustain itself?"[140]

Those questions surface a notion paradoxical to old leadership playbooks. Forged leaders don't control through a steep hierarchy. Rather, they strengthen their organizations through nurturing individuals' identity and ability to make decisions and create outcomes. The choice is this: Are you the sole winner, alone on the island leading no one? Or are you a leader who builds sustainable communities whose members help each other? *Hint: If you choose the former when you win—you lose.*

COMMUNITIES AND HUMAN-AGENCY

Communities are built of individuals. Individuals require the power to think and act to bring that energy into a positive outcome for the group. Further, the group deepens its values through actions. These are similar to action communications, discussed in chapter 8, since the group's values can be expressed through word and deed.

If the message from the leaders in an organization says one thing, but the leaders' actions say another, the message in the actions usually wins. The organizational development

---

140 Ibid.

field calls this "espoused theories" versus "theories-in-use."[141] An espoused theory might be, "at this company, we have no tolerance for unethical behavior." But at closer examination, the theory-in-use—the basis of managers' actions—is more like, "we will look the other way if you bring in a large sale."

That scenario was represented in a study that polled a sample of five thousand sales managers throughout the United States. The results showed greater leniency for high-performing salespeople with infractions than weaker sales performers.[142] Conversely, the closer what you say and what you do align, the more your values are transparent as they are put into action. Another study shows that when sales managers develop interpersonal relationships with their sales staff, a bridge of trust and empathy develops, and salespeople's actions become more ethical.[143]

―――♦―――

How do Forged leaders weave individual and organizational energies in volatile times? One element connected all the Forged Leaders' community-building stories—*human-agency*. Human-agency is a person's ability to see that their actions come from their own intentions and that they have the ability to bring change to their environment. Further, the

---

141 Donald Schön, *Educating the Reflective Practitioner*. San Francisco, CA: Jossey-Bass, 1987.

142 Joseph A. Bellizzi, and Ronald W. Hasty. "Supervising Unethical Sales Force Behavior: How Strong Is the Tendency to Treat Top Sales Performers Leniently?" *Journal of Business Ethics* 43, no. 4 (April, 2003): 337–51.

143 Raj Agnihotria, and Michael T. Krush. "Salesperson Empathy, Ethical Behaviors, and Sales Performance: The Moderating Role of Trust in One's Manager," *Journal of Personal Selling & Sales Management* 35, no. 2 (2015): 164–74.

ability for people to influence their outcomes also supports their sense of dignity.[144]

When instability hits a team, as when the group's members are displaced during a pandemic or stunned by a merger and acquisition, the team hunts for equilibrium at individual and group levels. These times of growth and transformation can raise valid questions of survival. "What are we going to do next? Will they separate us? Am I going to lose my job?"[145,146]

One way to respond when facing these types of safety and stability questions is through what might be called *good enough leadership*. This plays off child psychologist Donald Winnicott's idea of *good enough*. Being good enough means you're there to support the development of those you're responsible for and care about. You attend to that tender area that supports their developmental challenges and allow them to grow from their success and failures.[147]

In Winnicott's research, the parent figure performs a transitionary role in "potential space." This is an area to experiment, have fun, and play. "It is play that is the universal,"

---

144 Daniel A. Hojman and Álvaro Miranda, "Agency, Human Dignity, and Subjective Well-Being," *World Development* 101, 2018: 1–15.

145 Nancy Arenas and Tara Silver-Malyska, "Imagining the Unimaginable: Best Practices for Returning to Work Post-COVID-19," *Benefits Quarterly* 31, no. 1 (2021): 45–56.

146 Rekha Rao-Nicholson, Zaheer Khan, and Peter Stokes. "Making Great Minds Think Alike: Emerging Market Multinational Firms' Leadership Effects on Targets' Employee Psychological Safety after Cross-Border Mergers and Acquisitions," *International Business Review* (2016): 103–13.

147 Winnicott, D. W., *Playing and Reality,* London, UKs: Taylor & Francis, 2017.

Winnicott tells us.[148] Play centers on communication and contributes to health, growth, and group relationships.

Think of a child going to nursery school for the first time. The parent figure can't stay in the classroom with their child, but they can teach them skills they can take to school. We can tell them things like, "It's okay to speak up for yourself. Enjoy trying new things." Along with encouraging words, a physical object like a loved toy or doll can act as a transitional object—something the child brings into the room to nurture safety and grounding.

Forged leaders similarly understand that they cannot experience the discomfort of the unknown for their group. They allow their community to experience their struggles and move through them rather than deny them. Of course, that doesn't mean the leaders are not working toward the resolution of a problem. Rather they also appreciate the work the community members do in moving toward the resolution and work toward providing an environment where the team can feel safe to try new ideas.

As seen in the below Forged stories, the magical paradox of growing an individual's human-agency while building a community lies in creating that space for individuals to bloom. The stories that follow show human-agency leadership in three ways:

- **Fostering:** Leaders create community through nurturing the human-agency of community members

---

148 Ibid, p.56.

- **Bootstrapping:** Individuals emerge as leaders through the action of creating community
- **Adapting:** Leaders adapt a community to new situations by tapping into their own human-agency to establish change. This has the endless potential of forging new leaders within an established group.

These stories show powerful ways of approaching community building in physical as well as remote or online space. They also illuminate the payoffs community building can have for you as a leader and those you lead.

FOSTERING: KELLY AHN

Kelly Ahn's new role as Executive Director and later Associate Dean of the Career Center for the Columbia University School of Professional Studies started in March 2020, just as COVID-19 pushed her entire team to work remotely. Her office building closed the week before her start date, so she hadn't physically met her staff. One of her first actions was to meet the team through lengthy one-on-one calls. Even though she has extensive experience in leading these types of work groups, having everyone working remotely changed the dynamics. She decided to research different leadership styles to determine how best to provide the necessities of this newly displaced group and examined what type of leadership she would bring to this new environment.

Underlying her dedication to being a good leader is a passion for empathy and creativity propelled by her values. "I always felt like part of my identity I was born with [was] to walk on this path to help folks whether that was Korean immigrants or whether that was high school kids or LGBTQ or whatever cohort. I always felt I needed to help and support, and that empathy always drove all of my work." These values developed in part from her family, led by a Christian pastor, and from her own experience as an immigrant in Queens, New York, at the age of fifteen.

Bringing that personal connection to her work helped move her toward building human-agency in her staff. Together with human resources, the supervisors above her, her direct staff, and a team trauma consultant, she created an online retreat to focus on the pain the team had gone through. This helped the team process their experience and showed, through action, the appreciation of their voice.

This unique form of concern for the team shows the level of creativity Kelly brings to her work. Similarly, Kelly's leadership style is borne from her heart. It developed in part from her early days in Queens, "…trying to survive as an immigrant, knowing the sort of challenges of being an immigrant: the language barrier, being a woman, being a person of color, all of those things really helped me to be resourceful and innovative. And I think those things really helped me shape my being as a person." That creativity, aligned with her compassion for her team, translated directly into her model of flexible leadership that brought positive change to her staff.

Instead of fixing on one style of leadership, Kelly openly continued to reflect on and rebalance her leadership style, "showing my vulnerability, being very transparent about who I am and what I'm about." She even shared with her team what leadership style she was using so they could recognize

"...whether I was trying to be more of an authentic leader or whether I am trying to be more process oriented..."

"There was so much ambiguity, and I found answers to everything that I wanted to do along the way by just listening to people or listening to myself."

This transparent and modulating leadership style worked well in bringing her group into a successful community whose members support each other. Kelly works in the trenches with them, and they return the effort. "So, in all cases, it has always been my team members who were the biggest cheerleaders. They deliver the work with me, but I was always on the ground with them. And, at times, they really didn't see me as a leader but like somebody who's carrying this thing together. And I enjoy it that way."

BOOTSTRAPPING: NAIMEESHA MURTHY AND ASHLEE WISDOM

These are the stories of Naimeesha Murthy and Ashlee Wisdom, two entrepreneurs who did not set out with the intention to be great leaders. They proved themselves to be great leaders by filling a community need defined by their experience. They both formed online communities, which within a few years, grew exponentially.

Products by Women (productsbywomen.com), the community started by Naimeesha, grew from fifty to 15,000 members in 120 countries in its first 1.5 years. *Health In Her HUE* (healthinherhue.com), created by Ashlee, has seen its membership grow from about 300 members to 2,100 in a year's time. The statistics represent actively engaged community members not unengaged click-throughs.

How do you grow such a loyal membership base, and how does the work transform you as a leader? *Hint—It's an adventure!*

PRODUCTS BY WOMEN

Six years ago, while completing a course at New York University, Naimeesha was scouted and hired for product marketing at World Education Services. This organization helps connect international students to higher education institutions in the United States and Canada. Naimeesha pivoted from a nontechnical role to a highly technical one in 2017. While seeking mentorship, she couldn't find any help within her company and decided to create her own support group.

"It's something I started to really solve a problem for myself, and that was to build a network. I am an immigrant [...], and I felt like I have so many friends, and I still don't have that professional network." So, how do you initiate an effort to build your network when all you have is the problem? You listen. Naimeesha recalls, "There was so much ambiguity, and I found answers to everything I wanted to do along the way by just listening to people or listening to myself."

Products by Women started with about fifteen people, and Naimeesha was concerned at the first meeting. "It was just going to be me." Flash forward, Products by Women membership has expanded to include women from all career levels.[149]

HEALTH IN HER HUE

Ashlee's journey began from a place of pain, suffering, and an unfortunate encounter with a doctor. Her TEDx talk, which discusses the experience, portrays the pain of her old work environment inflamed by racist harassment.[150]

In response to the workplace microaggressions, her body responded with a daily bout of hives. Ashlee's doctor prescribed an over-the-counter medicine, but the hives did not stop. It felt to Ashlee like this doctor was content with prescribing a medical solution based purely on the remediation of her outward symptoms. She didn't ask about Ashlee's home, work life, or any stressors that might be affecting her.

At the same time, Ashlee did not feel comfortable volunteering information about the stress emanating from her work environment. "If my doctor were a black woman, I probably would have voluntarily told her about what I was dealing with at work. But because she wasn't, I never thought to mention ..., 'Hey, I'm dealing with microaggressions. I'm being treated badly in the workplace because of my race.'"

---

149 "About Us—Products by Women," Products by Women, 2020, accessed August 1, 2021.

150 Ashlee Wisdom, *How Healthcare's Failures Fuel Innovation*. Podcast audio, TEDxWakefield 2020.

Ashlee took the bold step of resigning from her job, and once she was away from the arena of microaggressions, the hives immediately ceased. The experience raised her awareness that being from the same community could ease the communication between patients and doctors. Ashlee dedicated herself to having more open, forthcoming communication with all her doctors going forward. She also saw the opportunity to bring help to others.

Ashlee created Health In Her HUE, a digital platform that connects Black women and women of color to culturally competent healthcare providers, health content, and community. She started with what she felt she could do on her own—create a website, write content, and develop the vision and mission statements. But she needed help since she was in graduate school, working full time, and couldn't write all the articles. So she posted the mission statement and vision on Facebook, and she tapped into her connections with healthcare professionals.

The response was overwhelming. "And so that's when I realized, okay, I'm onto something here. Because these people don't know me, but the mission and vision statement really resonated with them enough to want to write content for the platform." The membership quickly grew into the hundreds and expanded by nearly ten times during the pandemic.

ADAPTING: ROBIN LARKINS AND MARCELO TAIANO
At the top of the hill on Oak Street, the South Presbyterian church hails you as you pass through the main streets of

Dobbs Ferry, New York. The 1829 Gothic structure sits about twenty miles from the northern tip of Manhattan and houses the Dobbs Ferry Food Pantry. Before COVID-19 hit, they were providing food to thirty-five families a day. Within a week afterward, the families in need reached 185. All at once, their two eighty-year-old volunteer leaders had to press the pause button on their leadership roles, and the remaining volunteers had to assume leadership roles against a daily changing background.

Robin Larkins and Marcelo Taiano became the team co-leaders. Robin had previously been the Director of Cabrini Immigrant Services, also located in Dobbs Ferry. Marcelo volunteered at the food pantry and was one of the lead gardeners in the church's organic garden, which helps supply the food pantry.

In addition to the garden, the food pantry receives donations from various vendors, local farms, and larger food programs. During the pandemic, other types of businesses stepped up to fill the additional need. "[A local] restaurant in Dobbs Ferry delivered prepared foods for twenty weeks, and in that way, they kept some of their kitchen help working. We didn't pay them for that. They used some of what they had left in their stock rooms."

Robin and Marcelo faced an unending set of unexpected challenges, including being victims of their own success. Like the time they got so many food donations, they ran out of room to store them. They pounded the pavement (and the phones) and knocked on the doors of markets, restaurants, and farmers who responded. When we couldn't store vegetables, we would call local places and ask, 'do you have any refrigerator space left?' And we would run down there and put our lettuce or our broccoli in their refrigerator or freezer. So again, that responsiveness, it's kind of created this ripple effect we hope will continue beyond the crisis time."

The fast-paced changes the group endured led to challenges between the volunteers themselves. For example, there were conflicting opinions about whether they should be wearing masks or (in those early days of the pandemic) if they should save the masks for use by hospitals and other essential workers who were very short on personal protective equipment (PPE). They always wore masks and took precautions when handing out food. But when it was just volunteers working together, they had a hard time agreeing whether to wear masks.

Yet, without their regular leader, the team grew tighter by discovering their way forward together. For these types of issues, they found that a weekly debrief provided the answer. "We have regular Zoom meetings every Wednesday. Every volunteer is involved, and we voice our opinions on how things should be run, or if there's any kind of issue or if someone doesn't feel safe in any way." The organic way the Dobbs Ferry Food Pantry operates translates to their families in need through sustained access to meals.

TEACHINGS AND LEARNINGS
The first step to building communities emanates from the passion of recognizing a need in the world. These Forged leader stories of building communities reinforces this statement. They show that Forged leaders support a

community's development through strengthening its members' human-agency.

Community building is not a task for the faint of heart. It's demanding work. Accordingly, it's important to remember that Forged leaders do not have to and don't do this work alone.

Let's revisit the three ways that human-agency blooms by connecting them to their stories:

- **Fostering**–the story of Kelly Ahn exemplified how fostering human-agency amongst the community members can strengthen the entire community, supporting their personal and emotional needs while making the community stronger to accomplish their goals and be more innovative.
- **Bootstrapping**–through the stories of Naimeesha Murthy and Ashlee Wisdom, we saw how working on projects of passion can strengthen human-agency in leaders as they build communities. This is especially pronounced in communities where the leaders passionately felt a need or gap based on their own experience.
- **Adapting**–The story of Robin Larkins and Marcelo Taiano showed us how leaders could use their own human-agency and internal fortitude to help existing communities by adapting to new situations requiring new viewpoints or new skills.

LEVERAGE YOUR EXISTING COMMUNITIES

Naimeesha and Ashlee didn't grow into successful leaders by going it alone like cowhands on the open plains. They tapped into their extant communities to help them launch the new ones. This takes a strength that's found within vulnerability. In other words, Forged leaders reach out for help when they need it. They connect.

In fact, this notion appears in Naimeesha's concept of entrepreneurship. "You just have to be present at all times." And even though you might "feel exposed at times" or exhausted, "once you choose a path, your time is not yours alone, in a way." It's a dedication of spirit and action to the things you've chosen to commit to.

The digital community Ashlee created reflects the strong driving role that community plays in her work. She grew up as the first generation in a family of immigrants. The women in her family were hard workers who came to the United States with very little and built much more. They taught her the importance of providing support to those around you.

All the experiences of Ashlee's mentors, family, and church have shown her you need a community to accomplish things. That idea is reflected in the way Ashlee leads today. "I definitely want to make sure I make time supporting someone else coming behind me, even if I feel like I'm not that far along myself."

Ashlee and Naimeesha successfully grew communities that started with a passion emanating from their own experiences and from the wisdom that others can benefit from the communities they built. But it takes more than passion. It takes power to push through the fears, doubters, and unbeatable odds. It takes the support of a community.

TRUST YOURSELF

While Naimeesha spearheads Products by Women, she is clear the work is not about her ideas alone, "It's about how can we do this better." It's clear that growth is her most important goal when she says, "It's not about perfection. It's about progress." To illustrate, at one of the Products by Women online presentations, the key presenter had technical difficulties and could not connect. Naimeesha was not on the schedule to speak, but the presenter asked if she could jump in. "We had a lot of people there," Naimeesha said. "I was not prepared. I was not in the zone, and my son was crying in the background."

But she stepped up by telling herself, "You know what, I need to do this." And she did. "So, I switched on the camera, and I just jumped in and did it."

Naimeesha's story teaches us you have to trust yourself. Trust you are able to get through the fear and the uncertainty. Even if you don't know exactly how to come out of this thing, trust that you will. Then, build on that foundation of trust. Rationalize the problem by breaking it into achievable and understandable parts. Each of those parts is far more handleable than the whole.

Most importantly, you participate in a supportive network. If one does not exist, build it, starting with friends or family. It might start small, but you'll achieve your solution far more easily when you have a community that supports you, and you can support in return.

Ashlee created Health In Her HUE while completing her master's degree in Public Health Policy at New York University. "I remember reading an academic paper for a class late at night and getting emotional. I just remember being really disturbed and thinking, if I'm upset and bothered by these disparities, and this is something I just felt, if I feel burdened by it, I probably should do something. And I know I'm only one person. I can't change systemic racism, I can't change bias in the health care system, but I can do something to play a part and bring awareness to that. I can't do it all, but I can do something to work toward that."

Ashlee intends to expand her digital community to other women of color to enhance their health through community. Her current success is just the beginning. Health In Her HUE was born out of her frustrations with the gaps she observed in the health care community. And I anticipate her philosophy and impulses will drive her toward the solutions of other long-unsolved problems.

"We can see obstacles and failures for what they are at face value," Ashlee reminds us in her TEDx Talk, "or we can choose to see them as opportunities to improve, correct, and innovate." Her talk closes with hope and guidance by quoting from Brittney Cooper's *Eloquent Rage: A Black Feminist Discovers Her Superpower*, "May rage be a force for good because what you build is infinitely more important than what you tear down."[151,152]

---

151 Brittney Cooper, *Eloquent Rage: A Black Feminist Discovers Her Superpower*, New York, NY: St. Martin's Press, 2018.
152 Wisdom, How Healthcare's Failures Fuel Innovation, 2020.

NOT JUST FOR LEADERS

How do you become a leader who can wield the extraordinary power of communities? We opened this chapter with a reminder from Tom Chapin. "If you're the last survivor on the island, you're dead." Let's close with a story he told later in my 2011 interview with him.

Tom's brother Harry who founded World Hunger Year sadly died at age thirty-eight in a car accident on the Long Island highway. His death left a huge hole for his family, friends, and fans. James, the eldest Chapin brother, asked a question in his eulogy that all were thinking. How can they fill the hole left by Harry? How could they walk in his shoes?

James's response is a lesson for all leaders.

"None of us can be Harry. We wouldn't want to if we could. But what we can be, and what we can do is fill our own shoes a little fuller."[153]

Forged leaders walk into ambiguous dynamic situations, which none have seen before. They support people who need help and bring them together as a community. It's not a perfect science, and it's tough to come up with a quantitative statistic to show success. The real measure, though, is how you can fill your own shoes a little fuller.

---

153   Chapin, Talk About Things That Matter, 2011.

PART III

TEMPERING

CHAPTER 10

ALTERNATIVE WAYS TO BE A BETTER LEADER

"All of a sudden, overnight, this COVID situation hit us. And from a waitlist of one month, my practice suddenly disappeared, vanished into zero overnight—all patients canceled."

I was speaking with Amruta Inamdar about her physical therapy practice. She specializes in pelvic physical therapy, working with patients who are often in extreme pain. The work often requires physical manipulation along with exercises and stretches. Unfortunately, like many businesses, the pandemic lockdown shut down Amruta's practice in an instant.

But her patients' pain didn't cease with the lockdown. "At one end, people were struggling with this physical problem, but at the same time, they were also struggling with this emotional trauma of COVID." Emotional pain exacerbated her patients' physical pain. "The COVID situation was like a testimonial that there is definitely a mind-body connection."

Patients who were progressing well suddenly reached the highest level of pain due to stresses and the loss of family members from COVID-19.

The thing about volatile times is they can be scary, confusing, and a million other things, but at their base, they reflect one enduring truth...

Nothing stays the same.

How could Amruta adapt physical therapy into a remote model of healing over Zoom? Similar questions were asked by many helping businesses during the pandemic.

Beth Shaw, Founder and CEO at YogaFit Training Systems Worldwide, told me YogaFit had few online course offerings prior to COVID-19. "We had twenty-two and a half years of doing all live events, we were running fifteen conferences a year across North America, that typically got about 200–250 people in them, and we were also running almost 1,000 weekend trainings worldwide."

Then things rapidly changed, and YogaFit modified the playbook. "Literally within the span of two weeks from March 13 [2020], we were able to switch our entire business model to online, which is amazing."

Phoebe Leona, Founder of the nOMad Collective, a group that offers transformational experiences to become more embodied and empowered, also had to pivot when faced with the pandemic. She thought it was going to be challenging, and she succeeded by tapping into one of the collective's core values, "community, finding connection with others."

Phoebe told me, "We couldn't go around the world anymore. But we really had to go emphasize that exploring and taking that time to be quiet."

Seasonal changes also affected the nOMad Collective. "It shifted a little bit in the summertime. It was a bit of a challenge because everybody wanted to go outside. Now they got to be with people, but outside. And so that was something where I again had to make a pivot and say, 'Okay, let's quit online stuff for a minute, take the summer off, go do your thing. We'll see you in the fall.'"

This sense of leading a collective appears in other types of helping organizations. Angie Wojak, Director of Career Development at the School of Visual Arts, loves her work. "I think what I love is I get to kind of be a combination of a full-time agent and fan of the arts, and I get to dip in and out of a million kinds of artwork every day."

That kind of work requires a lot of travel to industry events and opening opportunities for the students. When the pandemic started, "Suddenly things [were] thrown up into the air. I had multiple trips planned between March and June. I was going to be in France, Hollywood, San Francisco, and all over the place."

When that changed, she viewed her options with a new perspective. "At first, you think, wow, look at all these lost opportunities. But actually, I think there's been a development of a sense of community and an openness to talk to people that didn't exist before." In fields that relied heavily on in-person interaction, Beth, Phoebe, and Angie responded to the dynamic pandemic environment and created new ways of helping their communities.

In a way, Forged leadership is the art of giving up all hope of finding the perfect way to lead and instead coming to terms with and responding to how you act as a leader in the situation that's in front of you.

Like other dedicated Forged leaders, Amruta created something unique to fit the situation. She tapped into the core value of her work, healing. Since she couldn't be with her patients, she taught them exercises she designed to do independently.

For her patients' stress, she added mindfulness meditation practices and restorative yoga, techniques that they would not normally have had time to do at the clinic. "From the physical therapy perspective, I was trying to cue them to mentally try and come in to answer the situation because if stress is overpowering you, especially with pelvic pain, or any kind of discomfort in the pelvic area that just compounds the problem." The results for her patients were so successful some continue to see her over Zoom. Amruta began to get requests globally from people with pelvic pain who were simultaneously dealing with emotional trauma.

Mindfulness not only had a positive impact on her clients. It also helped her move through the dramatic impact the pandemic had on her practice. First, it helped her bring a fresh view to the practice. "When there's an emergency, new doors open up. I feel like because I kept my mindfulness intact, I could see new opportunities through this."

Second, it helped her not only survive but thrive. "I mean, I could have easily become nervous, but instead, I looked at it as an opportunity, pivoted my business, and now I feel like I have new doors, new avenues to explore rather than just sticking to the one-on-one model."

In a way, Forged leadership is the art of giving up all hope of finding the perfect way to lead and instead coming to terms with and responding to how you act as a leader in the situation that's in front of you. Let's get a better sense of how mind, body, and heart play in the task of leadership.

INTENTION, INTUITION, AND BODY AWARENESS

Through the alternative lens, one way to tap into intuition is through intention. Setting an intention is both easy and difficult. *The difficult part* is thinking of intention not as setting end points and metrics but instead moving into the realm of awareness and possibility. To take that step, you have to relinquish the yearning for things to be other than they are and bring care to you and your team.

The easy part is everything you need is already inside you. Imagine intention falling within the realm of self-care.

Intentions can be something fundamental like, *I intend to hold an open heart and mind throughout the day,* or perhaps, *Today I intend to allow myself to notice and accept pleasant things that come to me.* Intentions allow you the openness to see your experience in new ways. Body awareness, or getting more in touch with body sensations through paying attention and listening to it, can provide additional information to help make decisions.[154]

EXPLORATION: TAPPING INTO INTUITION THROUGH BODY AWARENESS

For this exercise, we're going to check in on one of the things leaders rarely consider, yet which can highly inform their intuition—body awareness. The language of intuition incorporates the importance of body awareness. Think of the directive, "Listen to your gut."

Since each of us and each volatile moment is different, you may not always feel the intuitive answer in the gut. This exercise adds to your arsenal of decision-making techniques, as discussed in chapter 7—Go with Intuition—to help you tap into body sensations that can accompany your intuitive decisions.

Notice that intuition and listening to your gut are different from knee-jerk reactions to stimuli. Reactions are more tightly connected to ingrained survival reactions. Intuition works toward opening up awareness of what's happening

---

154 Jon Kabat-Zinn, *Full Catastrophe Living: Using the Wisdom of Your Body and Mid to Face Stress, Pain, and Illness,* New York, NY: Bantam Books, 2013.

right now. Try this exploration to let the body recognize what it feels like to make a decision that makes you proud.

This exploration is one of self-care. Modify the instructions in any way that assists you.

1. Sit in a chair and, as you are able, engage the intention of bringing your back into a straight and comfortable position.
2. Follow your breath as it flows in and out.
3. Continue for five or six repetitions. Focus on your breath. Notice any sensations associated with the breath. Is it perhaps warmer on the exhale than the inhale? Do you notice any other sensations?
4. Reflect on a time you made a time-bound decision you were proud of (one you had to complete by a specific date or time). Notice any other details that come to you about that decision. Were there worries? Celebrations? Do any aromas or sounds in the room enter the picture?
   a. Spend the time it takes for a few breaths in this remembrance.
5. Now scan your body for sensations (heartbeat, muscle, stomach, chest, whichever comes to your awareness).
   a. Once more, spend the length of a few breaths while you notice the sensations.
   b. What body sensations come to you as you are feeling proud of that decision?
6. When you are ready, bring your awareness back to this moment.
7. Jot down any body sensations you noticed in step five.
8. One more time, bring your awareness to the breath for a few repetitions as it flows in and out.

9. Now, bring your awareness to this moment, so you are fully awake and ready to move on with your day.

Reference your step seven notes of body sensations as you work with intuition and future decision-making. Just check in. "Hmm, if I go with my gut this time, it's telling me to do X." As an exercise, you can notice how your body speaks to you about decisions throughout the day. Eventually, when you're ready, try making low-impact decisions based on body sensations and see where the sensations lead you.

Now that you've investigated your internal process of intuition a bit, let's play with how flexibility and nonjudgment can work together to release you from perfectionism and surface your innovative abilities.

NONJUDGMENT, PATIENCE, AND PERFECTIONISM

Flexibility is core to innovative thinking and dealing with a crisis. We saw how this works in the stories of firefighters who quickly adapt their strategy when fighting wildfires.

Some concepts from meditation work can help build the path to flexibility. Beth Shaw reminded me, "I know from my own personal spiritual practice of meditation, the ultimate freedom is being connected to spirit. Because, when we connect to source consciousness, these bodies, we realize are very temporary." The mediation concepts can provide an awareness of your thoughts, body sensations, and emotions to help you see things differently. In a way, they allow you a chance to view situations from a variety of perspectives.

NONJUDGMENT

Letting go of judgment is a never-ending process. It's liberating yourself from habitual likes, dislikes, and opinions that can block you from opening to new perspectives. Likes and dislikes formed through habitual thinking—or "habits of mind"—incline us to make decisions and take actions based on assumptions and prejudgments.[155] This is similar to the success paradox discussed in chapter 2, The Learning Foundry, where we act by habit rather than by attending to what is happening at this moment right now.

PATIENCE

Patience is one of nonjudgment's siblings. It rests in accepting that sometimes things just need to happen in their own time. Patience can be elusive. You won't find it in giving in or giving up but instead in simply appreciating and accepting that some things have their own flow and growth speed (sometimes faster, sometimes slower). In chapter 8, Employ Action Communications, we saw how patience helped free Shailagh Murray to lead her team at Columbia University with a growth mindset by allowing her team to discover ways of using their skills in new and updated ways.

If impatience is driving you (perhaps into the ground), mindfulness can be a way to become aware of and observe what is behind your impatience (fear, desire, immediate crisis).[156]

---

155 Jack Mezirow, "Learning to Think Like an Adult: Core Concepts of Transformation Theory," In *Learning as Transformation: Critical Perspective on a Theory*, edited by Jack Mezirow and Associates. San Francisco, CA: Josey-Bass, 2000, 17–18

156 Kabat-Zinn, *Full Catastrophe Living*, 2013, p.23.

The same is true for you in your mindfulness practice. Patience without judgment is a gift of openness and space that you can practice for yourself. The "without judgment" part of that sentence is one of the toughest since judgment's relatives—pursuits and perfection—often propel us.

PERFECTIONISM

Perfection can be useful as a principle, for example, when the Zero Suicide Alliance created a community and methods to prevent suicide. Their guidance, which has proven to be effective, stems from the motto, "Suicide is preventable."[157,158]

You must take care in the pursuit of perfection. It is possible to slip into *clinical perfectionism*, where anything but absolute success is perceived as failure. Clinical perfectionism can result in self-harm, including eating disorders and suicide.[159,160]

One instrument that attempts to measure an individual's self-assessment of perfectionism is *The Frost Multidimensional Perfectionism Scale*. The instrument asks the individual to rate their agreement with statements like: "If I do not

---

157 "About Us," Zero Suicide Alliance, 2021, accessed September 5, 2021

158 David W. Covington and Michael F. Hogan, "Zero Suicide: The Dogged Pursuit of Perfection in Health Care," *Psychiatric Times* 36, no. 1 (2019): 16–17.

159 Paul l. Hewitt, Carmen F. Carlian, Chang Chen, and Gordon L. Flett, "Perfectionism, Stress, Daily Hassles, Hopelessness, and Suicide Potential in Depressed Psychiatric Adolescents," *Journal of Psychopathology and Behavioral Assessment* 36 (2014): 663–74.

160 Julie Scelfo, "Suicide on Campus and the Pressure of Perfection," *New York Times* July 27, 2015.

set very high standards for myself, I am likely to end up a second-rate person, and people will probably think less of me if I make a mistake."[161]

Shigetaka Komori, former Chairman and CEO of Fujifilm, whom we discussed in chapter 3, From Disruption to Resilience, considered perfection in his leadership role. "When I became CEO, I wanted to be like an all-powerful force with infallible judgment. I knew, too, that perfection is a futile pursuit."[162] Komori went on to lead Fujifilm to win the battle of digital cameras over Kodak.

Forged leadership is a messy process without perfect answers. Softening to nonjudgment and patience can be a powerful antidote to moments where you are not able to uphold your own impossible standards of perfection.

EXPLORATION: RESPONDING TO THE CALL OF PERFECTION
In this short exploration, you can experiment with responding to the call of perfection with nonjudgment and patience.

Remember to exercise self-care in this exploration and alter the steps in any way that assists you.

1. Find a quiet space of your own.

---
161 Gordon L. Flett and Paul L. Hewitt, "Measures of Perfectionism," Chap. 21 In *Measures of Personality and Social Psychological Constructs*, edited by Gregory J. Boyle, Donald H. Saklofske and Gerald Matthews, 595–618, London, UK: Academic Press, 2015, p.600.
162 Komori, Innovating out of Crisis, 2013, p.135.

2. Sit in a chair and, as you are able, engage the intention of bringing your back into a straight and comfortable position.
3. Follow your breath as it flows in and out. Continue for four or five repetitions.
4. Close your eyes or bring them to a soft gaze toward the floor a few feet in front of you.
5. Now, notice the breath as you inhale. Observe it all the way to the bottom of the breath, wherever that rests in your body—your lungs, torso, belly. Notice any temperature changes or any other attributes of the breath as it flows in and out. Just noticing and allowing it.
6. Acknowledge any sounds that come into your awareness.
7. Now move your awareness back to the breath. Just watch your breath as you breathe in and breathe out.
8. Next, acknowledge any desires or goals that might pass through your awareness. Just allow them to be without wishing they were different or trying to achieve them.
9. Allow these desires or goals to float on like clouds as you bring your attention back to your breath, following your breath as you inhale and exhale, and perhaps consider this quote from Ram Dass. "Perfected beings rest in emptiness… Out of [this restful place] comes the optimum response to any life situation."[163]
10. Now, slowly open your eyes and bring your awareness to this moment, so you are fully awake and ready to move on with your day.

---

163 Ram Dass, *Be Love Now: The Path of the Heart*. New York, NY: HarperCollins, 2010, p.103.

Check in with how this exploration was for you. How was it to play with the notion of allowing goals to just be and perhaps pass by without latching on to them? Did you find comments or rumination flow into your awareness? If so, next time you try these steps, see how it feels to allow those comments simply to be. By allowing your goals of perfection to be, it may be possible, even for just a moment, to loosen their grip.

CHAPTER 11

CONCLUSION

I love the cooking competition show *Chopped*, where chefs skillfully adapt surprise ingredients into amazing dishes. You can almost smell the dishes through the screen. The judges often comment about a dish's cohesiveness or how all the elements work together. You could have a plate of three great components, but without something such as a sauce tying them together, the plate doesn't work, and you're chopped out of the competition. In writing this book, I was lucky to find my cohesive element early on. I've mentioned it several times, and it stems directly from a *Financial Times* interview with Eric Yuan, CEO of Zoom. When Eric was a boy, his father instilled in him the values "hard work and stay humble."[164]

Those values moved my writing forward and appeared across the Forged leader stories as the more specific six practices of great leadership in volatile times. I wasn't sure exactly what I would find with the initial interviews, but what quickly emerged was the overarching work of compassion and community.

---

164 Eric Yuan, a Tech Boss Riding a Geopolitical Storm, Financial Times, 2020.

COMPASSION AND COMMUNITY

"Our human compassion binds us the one to the other," Nelson Mandela said, "not in pity or patronizingly, but as human beings who have learnt how to turn our common suffering into hope for the future."[165]

As we've seen, Forged leaders absolutely care about how their actions impact the well-being of the individuals and organizations they lead. Compassionate leadership binds individuals and communities.

This was impressively revealed, for example, in Kelly Ahn's approach to bringing her team together in her new position, even though she had yet to see them in person, or when Virginia Gambale led a major US domestic airline into the age of onboard Wi-Fi. It's seen in Peter Koletzke's role as stage manager, rectifying an extreme lighting problem during a live dance performance, and in David Clarke's intuitive decision to make an unplanned fuel stop to prevent an emergency landing.

HUMILITY AND LEARNING

Like Kodak clinging to their core competency of film past its expiration date, the voices of command and control as an everyday leadership technique are, for the most part, the dying gasps of entropy. The component of humility tells us so. Humility shows that we need to keep an open mind. We don't know everything and can't control everything. It recognizes

---

[165] Nelson Mandela, *Notes to the Future: Words of Wisdom*, New York, NY: Atria Books, 2012, p.24.

the futile search for ultimate control and welcomes us into the realm of learning, open-mindedness, and innovation. While we might dream of a new normal, humility signifies normal is just one more step on the path of change to the *next normal*.

That's why it's so important to constantly be viewing Forged leaders' work. They deal with what's happening right in the moment. Some of the book's stories took place years back and some months back. And we can find leaders that exhibit Forged leader qualities in the past, present, and future. The lessons are timeless because, while Forged leaders might take lessons from the past, they know and act on what's happening right in front of them. This is true whether they're dealing with a sudden emergency or planning strategy for the future.

While we might dream of a new normal, humility signifies normal is just one more step on the path of change to the *next normal*.

President John F. Kennedy had prepared a speech to deliver on November 22, 1963, to the Dallas Citizens Council. That same afternoon he met his tragic death. The undelivered speech contains an understanding of how important learning is to leaders. One could have written that speech specifically for today's leaders.

"This link between leadership and learning is not only essential at the community level. It is even more indispensable in world affairs. In a world of complex and continuing problems, in a world full of frustrations and irritations, America's leadership must be guided by the lights of learning and reason, or else those who confuse rhetoric with reality and the plausible with the possible will gain the popular ascendancy with their seemingly swift and simple solutions to every world problem."[166]

Leaders have to deal with reality by learning what's truly going on in the world they lead.

HARD WORK AND TAKING ACTION

Finally, let's talk about hard work. We often picture hard work as the application of elbow grease or working long hours, a high level of effort, perseverance, and perhaps self-sacrifice. For Forged leaders, it may be easier to define by looking outside the realm of leadership. In a 1956 textbook on how hard it is to study, schoolmaster William Armstrong provides a definition of studying that works well to understand hard work. "Total of all the habits, determined purposes, and enforced practices that the individual uses [to get the job done]."[167]

Hard work harkens to Eric Yuan's Zoom inspiration story. In 1994 he saw Bill Gates present the possibilities of the internet to an audience in Japan.[168] An inspired Yuan launched

---

166 John F. Kennedy, "Undelivered Remarks for Dallas Citizens Council, Trade Mart, Dallas, Texas, 22 November 1963," Dallas Citizens Council, Trade Mart, Dallas, TX, John F. Kennedy Presidential Library and Museum, November 22, 1963.

167 William Howard Armstrong, *Study Is Hard Work*. New York, NY: Harper & Brothers, 1956, p.2.

168 "A Bill Gates Speech Inspired Zoom Founder to Start an Internet Business—Now He's a Billionaire," CNBC: Make It, CNBC.com, Updated August 3, 2021.

eight attempts within the next two years to acquire a visa to the United States. "I told myself, okay, great. I'll do all I can until you tell me that I can never come here anymore. Otherwise, I'm not going to stop."[169] And he didn't stop until he finally reached the United States, where he eventually landed a job with WebEx, a competitive remote meeting service now owned by Cisco.

Leaving WebEx to found the competitor Zoom was such a leap that he found it hard to rally others behind his vision. Investors and friends put in 250,000 dollars, but their faith was shaky. "Everyone in venture capital thought it was a terrible idea," said Jim Scheinman, one of Zoom's initial venture investors.[170] Yuan told his wife, "I know it's a long journey and very hard, but if I don't try it, I'll regret it."[171] When Yuan publicly admitted the mistakes the company made during the tremendous Zoom expansion in 2020, the journey seemed to harken back to his father's guidance to use both hard work and humility.

YOUR STORY

Yes, Forged leaders work hard. They take the totality of their ways, learned through experiences and transformations, their determination to be the best leaders they can be for their team and their organization, and the lessons they learned along the way and turn them into action.

---

[169] "Zoom, Zoom, Zoom! The Exclusive inside Story of the New Billionaire Behind Tech's Hottest IPO," Forbes, Forbes Media, Updated August 2, 2021.

[170] Ibid.

[171] Ibid.

The F.O.R.G.E.D. acronym is a quick way to remember the practices to use as a leader in volatile times:

- **F**avor Compassion
- **O**wn the Unexpected
- **R**ecast Ideas
- **G**o with Intuition
- **E**mploy Action Communications
- **D**rive Community Bonds

Here's another shorthand that groups the six practices together to use when making decisions and taking action. Remember these three Cs:

- **Concentration:** bringing your awareness to the present moment, to be fully aware of the situation and its context (the power structures, timelines, history, meaning of the situation).
- **Curiosity:** bringing an open mind, free of prejudgment, yet ready to bring expertise and experience in designing new solutions. This could happen in an instant or as long as needed, given an honest understanding of the current situation.
- **Compassion:** bringing your concern for the well-being of others and yourself to bear on decisions and actions. Compassion exists in the creation of personal connections and community and exhibits through the values you bring to bear on the situation.

"Don't catch on fire! Don't wear clothing that melts!"[172] These warnings to beginner blacksmiths scream with danger. Yet blacksmiths continue to work with metal. You are now the blacksmith, and you are also the process and the result. Like a blacksmith, you are dynamic and adjust your works as you build, transforming your metal throughout.

The Forged leaders didn't know when they moved through the Forge that they were creating stories. But in telling the stories, they shine. Now that you have heard from the them, it's time to create your own Forged leader stories. Maybe someday they'll be told in writing or song, but they will definitely be told through the actions of those you've led.

Consider what you want your story to be. Start writing it now.

---

[172] Garon Power, "What Do You Really Need to Wear When You Blacksmith?" *Blacksmithing Basics*. Blacksmithing Basics, 2021.

GLOSSARY

Facilitative Leader: Leaders that create the conditions that facilitate the emergence of innovation (In chapter 2)

Forged Leaders: Individuals who are called to lead during volatile times (In chapter 1)

Intelligent Risk: A decision or risk assessment performed by using the best information you can get a hold of and balancing it with your experience and values. It recognizes that every decision has some risk level to it. (In chapter 7)

Meaning of Purpose: Five components highlighted by John Dewey of moving from observing something to responding to it. (In chapter 7)

Resilient Change: When something new has occurred or you create something new, innovators need to make a fast pivot in thought and action to make use of it or to respond to it. (In chapter 3)

Resilient Transformation: Resilient transformation encompasses both resilient change and resilient transition. Its pace and level of resistance are unpredictable. (In chapter 3)

Resilient Transition: Resilient transition represents a turning point based on long-term strategy. It is often characterized by a slower pace and less resistance. (In chapter 3)

S-curve: A predictive indicator for life cycles across a variety of fields like nature or business. (In chapter 5)

Traditional Leader: Traditional leaders serve as a standard of what to strive for in vision, values, and goals. (In chapter 2)

Volatile Times: Moments that require decisions in the face of ambiguity, when the outcome of those decisions and associated actions have a high impact on organizations and people's lives. (See Forged Leaders) (In chapter 1)

BOOK RELATED WEBSITES

Amazon (*amazon.com*)

The Animation Workshop at VIA University College (*animationworkshop.via.dk*)

Columbia University (*columbia.edu*)

Dobbs Ferry Food Pantry (*dobbsferrypantry.org*)

Douglas Scherer (*douglasscherer.com*)

Dr. Amruta Inamdar Pelvic Floor Physical Therapy (*dramrutainamdar.com*)

Fujifilm (*global.fujifilm.com*)

General Motors (*gm.com*)

Health In Her HUE (*healthinherhue.com*)

JetBlue (*jetblue.com*)

Julia Sloan (*www.sloaninternationalconsulting.com*)

Kodak (*kodak.com*)

LEGO (*lego.com*)

Li & Fung (*lifung.com*)

MIT Artificial Intelligence Laboratory (*csail.mit.edu*)

Murray Louis Dance Company (*pbs.org/wnet/americanmasters/murray-louis-about-murray-louis, https://youtu.be/REdwpR2Z9Nc*)

The nOMad Collective (*nomadalwaysatom.com*)

Nutanix (*nutanix.com*)

Products By Women (*productsbywomen.com*)

Rebecca Reynolds (*instagram.com/rebeccareynoldsresiliency*)

School of Visual Arts (*sva.edu*)

The Transformation Group (*thetransformationgroup.io*)

YogaFit Worldwide (*yogafit.com*)

Zero Suicide Alliance (*zerosuicidealliance.com*)

Zoom (*zoom.us*)

ACKNOWLEDGMENTS

Thanks so much to my family, who helped make this a wild and joyful voyage. Primary thanks go to my lovely wife Nélida, a highly accomplished writer and researcher in her own right who suffered my endless mini writing questions throughout the entire process. Thanks also for her translation of the Antonio Machado poem in chapter 8. My amazing daughter Juliana, also an achieved writer, gets top tier thanks as well. She got stuck repeatedly with questions like, "What word would you use here?"

Great thanks to my mother Helene, Aunt Jackie, and the rest of my family Bob, Evan, Jennifer, Melanie and Renee for their encouragement in pulling this project together.

I have such supportive friends, and one particularly stands out as a major contributor and influencer to this work. In addition to being a friend and professional colleague, Peter Koletzke has performed what the publisher calls "heavy pen editing." Thanks, Peter (and to your heavy pen), for your important contributions.

I was fortunate that Leslie Tierstein provided an in-depth editorial review of the full manuscript. Her work corrected and smoothed the writing to make it a far better reading experience. Leslie also edited my first two books, which were popular in their field and later translated into two other languages. Thank you, Leslie, for your no-holds-barred suggestions. Here's to another successful book!

The Forged leader stories give this manuscript wings. Thanks to all the Forged interviewees for their generous offering of time, stories, and support for this project.

Amurta Inamdar
Angie Wojak
Ashlee Wisdom
Beth Shaw
David Clarke
Julia Sloan
Kathy Schreiner
Kelly Ahn
Lotte Kronborg Thomsen
Marcelo Taiano
Naimeesha Murthy
Peter Koletzke
Phoebe Leona
Rebecca Reynolds
Robin Larkins
Sethretta Frank
Shailagh Murray
Sunil Notani
Virginia Gambale

The production side of this book includes the efforts of so many individuals. Thanks to my development editor Cassandra Caswell-Stirling who helped drag the core writing out of my brain and into the first draft. Much thanks to Eric Koester, Founder of the Creator Institute, and Brian Bies, Head of Publishing at New Degree Press, who bookended the teaching and strategy of the entire process. How they have time to respond to my individual questions is a mystery to solve in its own book. Thanks to my marketing editor Kristy Carter, my author coaches Haley Newlin, John Saunders, Kyra Ann Dawkins, and Stephen Howard who provided fantastic (sometimes wild) ideas to move the work forward and get the message out, and to my author accountability partner Heidi Torres for helping me keep centered and motivated.

I need to give a shout-out to my seriously impressive master's students, graduates, and faculty colleagues. Thank you for continually teaching me. I am very fortunate our paths met.

Thank you to Kae Bara Kratcha, a superior research librarian who pointed me in rewarding directions to find resources. Thanks to the Fondation Antonio Machado, Collioure who helped in confirming the public domain status of the Antonio Machado poem in chapter 8. Thanks also to Michelle Melani at Kappa Delta Pi who unearthed the details of the 1938 John Dewey lecture. Special thanks to Kenny Suleimanagich who helped me secure an official scan of his Master's Thesis, containing in vivo interviews with former Kodak executives for use in this book.

A special thanks to my supporters who helped me turn these ideas into an actual book during the prelaunch campaign.

The author community we have created truly helped through this journey.

Albina Zaripova
Amy Rae
Anonymous
Bartholomew Perez
Begoña Pino
Buck Moore
Carmela Bennett
Charryse Johnson
Chris Torres
Carrie Shockley
Coonoor Behal
David C. Clarke
Diego Valdés
Eric Koester
Evan Scherer
Heidi Torres
Helen Remotti
Jerry Julian
Jimmy Etimos
Jin Hi Rheem
John Sterling
Julia Sloan
Kathy Schreiner
Dr. Kayvon K
Louis Waweru
Marcelo Taiano
Musah Ali
N. Quintero
Naimeesha Murthy

Nicole Arndt
Olga Cooperman
Patricia Lee
Philip Reeves
Phoebe Miller
Robert and Mini Quigley
Robert F. Scherer
Robert Montay
Roque Martinez
Rosaura Bollengier
Sugee Kim
Sunil Notani
Tamara DaCosta
Theresa B. Skaar
Turgay Mehmet
Virginia Gambale
Yuran Qiu

WORKS CITED

INTRODUCTION

Figueroa-González, Javier. "Manager's Leadership Styles and Employee Engagement: Quantifying Manager's Influence." PhD, School of Education, Capella University. 2011.

Kahn, William A. "Psychological Conditions of Personal Engagement and Disengagement at Work." *The Academy of Management Journal* 33 (4): 692–724. 1990.

May, Douglas R., Richard L. Gilson, and Lynn M. Harter. "The Psychological Conditions of Meaningfulness, Safety and Availability and the Engagement of the Human Spirit at Work." *Journal of Occupational and Organizational Psychology* 77: 11–37. 2004.

CHAPTER 1

Chriscaden, Kimberly. "Impact of COVID-19 on people's livelihoods, their health and our food systems: Joint statement by ILO, FAO, IFAD and WHO" World Health Organization. 2020. *https://www.who.int/news/item/13-10-2020-impact-of-covid-19-on-people's-livelihoods-their-health-and-our-food-systems.*

Jernberg, John. *Forging; Manual of Practical Instruction in Hand Forging of Wrought Iron, Machine Steel, and Tool Steel; Drop Forging; and Heat Treatment of Steel, Including Annealing, Hardening, and Tempering.* Chicago, IL: American Technical Society, p.97. 1918.

National Transportation Safety Board. *Aircraft Accident Report: Loss of Thrust in Both Engines After Encountering a Flock of Birds and Subsequent Ditching on the Hudson River Us Airways Flight 1549 Airbus A320-214, N106US Weehawken, New Jersey, January 15, 2009.* National Transportation Safety Board (Washington, DC). May 4, 2010

Vlasic, Bill, and Matthew L Wald. "G.M. Expands Ignition Switch Recall to Later Models." *The New York Times*, March 29, 2014, B1, 4.

Putre, Laura. "The Barra Era: A Look Back and What's Ahead for Gm." *IndustryWeek*. 2020.

CHAPTER 2

Capra, Fritof. *The Hidden Connections: Integrating the Biological, Cognitive, and Social Dimensions of Life into a Science of Sustainability.* New York, NY: Double Day. 2002.

Deth, Richard C. *Molecular Origins of Human Attention the Dopamine-Folate Connection.* New York, NY: Springer Science+Business. 2003.

Eisenhower, Dwight D. *Public Papers of the Presidents of the United States, Dwight D. Eisenhower, 1957: Containing the Public Messages, Speeches, and Statements of the President, January 1 to December 31, 1957.* College Park, MD: General Services Administration, National Archives and Records Service, Federal Register Division. 1958.

Marvin, Caroline Braun. "How Curiosity Drives Actions and Learning: Dopamine, Reward, and Information Seeking." Doctor of Philosophy, Graduate School of Arts and Sciences, Columbia University. 2016.

Nonaka, Ikujiro. "Toward Middle-Up-Down Management: Accelerating Information Creation." *Sloan Management Review* 9 (3): 9–18. 1988.

Petraeus, David H. David Petraeus on Strategic Leadership. In *Belfer Center for Science and International Affairs*, edited by Emile Simpson. Cambridge, MA: Belfer Center for Science and International Affairs. 2016.

Sapolsky, Robert M. *Why Zebras Don't Get Ulcers*. New York, NY: Holt Paperbacks.

Dailymotion Editors. "Dopamine Jackpot! Sapolsky on the Science of Pleasure" (Lecture). Dailymotion.com. 2004.

Scherer, Douglas. "Levinson's Dream Theory and Its Relevance in an Academic Executive Mentoring Program: An Exploratory Study of Executive Mentors' Practice and Individuation." Ed.D., Organizational Leadership and Learning, Columbia University. 2010.

Sloan, Julia. *Learning to Think Strategically*. 4th ed. New York, NY: Routledge. 2020.

Tedeschi, Ellen. "Knowledge for the Sake of Knowledge: Understanding the Relationship between Curiosity, Exploration, and Reward." Doctor of Philosophy, Graduate School of Arts and Sciences, Columbia University. 2020.

CHAPTER 3

Ballard, John. "If You Invested $500 in Amazon's IPO, This Is How Much You'd Have Now." *The Motley Fool*. https://www.fool.com/investing/2019/11/24/if-you-invested-500-in-amazons-ipo-this-is-how-muc.aspx. 2019.

Bezos, Jeffrey P. *Amazon.Com Annual Report—1997*. Amazon.com (Seattle, WA). 1997.

Bughin, Jacques, and Nicolas van Zeebroeck. "The Case for Offensive Strategies in Response to Digital Disruption." iCite-International Centre for Innovation, Technology and Education Studies, Bruxelles, Belgium. https://ftp.zew.de/pub/zew-docs/veranstaltungen/Presaentation.pdf. 2017.

Christensen, Clayton M. "The Innovator's Challenge: Understanding the Influence of Market Environment on Processes of Technology Development in the Rigid Disk Drive Industry." Doctor of Business Administration Dissertation, Graduate School of Business Administration, Harvard University. 1992.

Christensen, Clayton M., and Karen Dillon. "Disruption 2020: An Interview with Clayton M. Christensen." MIT Sloan Management Review. Accessed September 10, 2021. https://sloanreview.mit.edu/article/an-interview-with-clayton-m-christensen/. 2020.

Downes, Larry, and Paul F. Nunes. "Big-Bang Disasters." *Harvard Business Review* March 2013: 44–56. 2013.

Euchner, James, and Clayton M. Christensen. "Managing Disruption: An Interview with Clayton Christensen." *Research Technology Management* 54, no. January–February 2011 (1): 11–17. 2011.

Ho, Jonathan C., and Hongyi Chen. "Managing the Disruptive and Sustaining the Disrupted: The Case of Kodak and Fujifilm in the Face of Digital Disruption." *Review of Policy Research* 35 (3): 353–371. 2018.

Koester, Eric. Simon Sinek. In *Creator Institute*, edited by Eric Koester. Georgetown, DC: Creator Institute. 2021

Komori, Shigetaka. *Innovating out of Crisis: How Fujifilm Survived (and Thrived) As Its Core Business Was Vanishing*. Berkeley, CA: Stone Bridge Press. 2013.

LEGO Company. *Annual Accounts 1999*. Lego (Billund, Denmark). 1999.

Lidz, Franz. "How Lego Is Constructing the Next Generation of Engineers." *Smithsonian Magazine* May 2013. https://www.smithsonianmag.com/innovation/how-lego-is-constructing-the-next-generation-of-engineers. 2013.

Proudfoot, Kekoa. "Reverse Engineering the Lego RCX." Kekoa Proudfoot. Last Modified December 13, 2020. http://www.mralligator.com/rcx/talk/. 1998.

Reynolds, Rebecca. Discussion on Resilience. Edited by Douglas Scherer.

Sandströmarchive, Christian. 2011. "You Press the Button. Kodak Used to Do the Rest." *MIT Technology Review*. 2020.

Sinek, Simon. *Start with Why: How Great Leaders Inspire Everyone to Take Action*. New York, NY: Portfolio/Penguin, p.79. 2009.

Suleimanagich, Kenny. "The Decline of a Giant: An inside Look at Kodak's Downfall." MS, School of Journalism, Columbia University. 2013.

US Copyright Office. The Digital Millennium Copyright Act of 1998: US Copyright Office Summary. Edited by US Copyright Office. Washington, DC: US Copyright Office. 1998.

Watters, Audrey. "Lego Mindstorms: A History of Educational Robots." Hack Education. Last Modified December 13, 2020. http://hackeducation.com/2015/04/10/mindstorms. 2015.

Yagnik, Arpan, and Yamini Chandra. "Using Creativity to Defeat Fear and Manage Ambiguity for Enhancing Entrepreneurial Decisions." In *The Anatomy of Entrepreneurial Decisions: Past, Present and Future Research Directions*, edited by Andrea Caputo and Massimiliano M. Pellegrini, In Contributions to Management Science, 9–28. Cham, Switzerland: Springer Nature. 2019.

CHAPTER 4

Decety, Jean, and Kalina J. Michalska. "Neurodevelopmental Changes in the Circuits Underlying Empathy and Sympathy from Childhood to Adulthood." *Developmental Science* 13 (6): 886–899. 2010.

Engström, Maria, and Birgitta Söderfeldt. "Brain Activation During Compassion Meditation: A Case Study." *The Journal of Alternative and Complementary Medicine* 16 (5): 597–599. 2010.

Freire, Paulo. *Pedagogy of the Oppressed*. New York: Herder and Herder. 1970.

Halla, Judith A., Rachel Schwartzb, and Fred Duonga. "How Do Laypeople Define Empathy." *The Journal of Social Psychology* 161 (1): 5–24. 2021.

Harry, Sasha. "Predictors of Burnout for Frontline Nurses in the Covid-19 Pandemic: Well-Being, Satisfaction with Life, Social Support, Fear, Work Setting Factors, Psychological Impacts, and Self-Efficacy for Nursing Tasks." Doctor of Education Dissertation, Teachers College, Columbia University. 2021.

Klimecki, Olga M., Susanne Leiberg, Claus Lamm, and Tania Singer. "Functional Neural Plasticity and Associated Changes in Positive Affect After Compassion Training." *Cerebral Cortex* 23 (7): 1552–1561. 2013.

Klimecki, Olga M., Susanne Leiberg, Matthieu Ricard, and Tania Singer. "Differential Pattern of Functional Brain Plasticity after Compassion and Empathy Training." *Social Cognitive and Affective Neuroscience* 9 (6): 873–879. 2014.

Koopmann-Holm, Birgit, and Jeanne L. Tsai. "Focusing on the Negative: Cultural Differences in Expressions of Sympathy." *Journal of Personality and Social Psychology* 107 (6): 1092–1115. 2014.

O'Brien, Sara Ashley. "Google X exec: We need to fail faster." CNN Business. Cable News Network. Last Modified July 26, 2021. https://money.cnn.com/2015/03/18/technology/google-x-astro-teller-sxsw/index.html. 2015.

Parks, Sharon Daloz, Laurent A. Parks Daloz, Cheryl H. Keen, and James P. Keen. *Common Fire: Leading Lives of Commitment in a Complex World*. Boston, MA: Beacon Press. 1997.

Ramchal, Tanuja. "Seven Lessons in Failing Forward from a Google Employee." Huffpost. Last Modified July 26, 2021. https://www.huffpost.com/entry/7-lessons-in-failing-forward-from-a-google-employee_b_9602924. 2017.

Shuck, Brad, Meera Alagaraja, Jason Immekus, Denise Cumberland, and Maryanne Honeycutt-Elliott. "Does Compassion Matter in Leadership?: A Two-Stage Sequential Equal Status Mixed Method Exploratory Study of Compassionate Leader Behavior and Connections to Performance in Human Resource Development." *Human Resource Development* 30: 537–564. 2019.

Simon-Thomas, Emiliana R., Jakub Godzik, Elizabeth Castle, Olga Antonenko, Aurelie Ponz, Aleksander Kogan, and Dacher J. Keltner. "An fMRI Study of Caring vs Self-Focus During Induced Compassion and Pride." *Social cognitive and affective neuroscience* 7 (6): 635–648. 2012.

Singer, Tania, and Olga M. Klimecki. "Empathy and Compassion." *Current Biology* 24 (18). 2014.

Strauss, Terry. Common Fire: Leading Lives of Commitment in a Complex World. 1996.

Todaro-Franceschi, Vidette. *Compassion Fatigue and Burnout in Nursing: Enhancing Professional Quality of Life.* New York, NY: Springer Publishing Company. 2013.

Trauernichta, Mareike, Elisa Oppermann, Uta Klusmannc, and Yvonne Anders. "Burnout Undermines Empathising: Do Induced Burnout Symptoms Impair Cognitive and Affective Empathy?" *Cognition and Emotion* 35 (1): 185–192. 2021.

Wang, Shelia. "A Conceptual Framework for Integrating Research Related to the Physiology of Compassion and the Wisdom of Buddhist Teachings." In *Compassion: Conceptualisations, Research, and Use in Psychotherapy*, edited by Paul Gilbert. New York, NY: Routledge. 2005.

CHAPTER 5

Ailworth, Erin. "California Firefighters Battle Exhaustion from Perpetual Blazes; Crews Go from One Wildfire to Another on Little Sleep; 'I'd Be Lying to You If I Didn't Say I Worry About Their Safety." *Wall Street Journal (Online); New York, N.Y.* November 19, 2018. 2018.

Bachmann, Andreas, and Britta Allgöwer. "Uncertainty Propagation in Wildland Fire Behaviour Modelling." *International Journal of Geographical Information Science* 16 (2): 115–127. 2002.

Bartolo, Kylie, and Brett Furlonger. "Leadership and Job Satisfaction among Aviation Fire Fighters in Australia." *Journal of Managerial Psychology* 15 (1): 97–93. 2000.

CAL FIRE. "2018 Statistics and Events" California Department of Forestry and Fire Protection. *https://www.fire.ca.gov/stats-events/*. 2018.

Kabat-Zinn, Jon. *Wherever You Go, There You Are: Mindfulness Meditation in Everyday Life.* New York, NY: Hyperion. 2005.

Kumar, V., and Anita Pansari. "Measuring the Benefits of Employee Engagement." *MIT Sloan Management Review* 56 (4): 67–72. 2015.

Langer, Arthur M. *Analysis and Design of Next-Generation Software Architectures: 5G, IoT, Blockchain, and Quantum Computing.* Cham, Switzerland: Springer. 2020.

Meyer, Robinson. "The Simple Reason That Humans Can't Control Wildfires." *Science* 322 (4). 2018.

"Forecasting the Rise and Fall of Almost Anything." *The Futurist* 28 (5): 20–25. 1994.

"An Examination of the Preferences for Leadership Style of Firefighters of Different Rank and Generational Cohort " PhD, Educational Human Resource Development, Texas A&M University. 2011.

Smith, Todd D., Franklin Eldridge, and David M. DeJoy. "Safety-Specific Transformational and Passive Leadership Influences on Firefighter Safety Climate Perceptions and Safety Behavior Outcomes." *Safety Science* 86: 92–97. 2016.

"How Connector Managers Create Star Performers." Smarter with Gartner. Gartner. https://www.gartner.com/smarterwithgartner/how-connector-managers-create-star-performers/. 2019.

CHAPTER 6

Inmarsat Aviation. "Making Quality Count: Bring It On." *Global White Paper*. 2018.

The Mandarin Superstar. In *The Pierre Berton Show*, edited by Pierre Berton. 1971.

Lutz, Antoine, Daniel R. McFarlin, David M. Perlman, Tim V. Salomons, and Richard J. Davidson. "Altered Anterior Insula Activation During Anticipation and Experience of Painful Stimuli in Expert Meditators." *NeuroImage* 64: 538–546. 2013.

Scherer, Douglas. "Using Reflective Learning in Information Technology Crisis Resolution." In *The Dark Side of Technological Innovation*, edited by Bing Ran, 231–254. Charlotte, NC: Information Age Publishing. 2012.

Terenzini, Patrick T. "On the Nature of Institutional Research" Revisited: Plus ça Change...?" *Research in Higher Education* 54 (2): 137–148. 2013.

"About the Cathedral-Cathedral of Saint John the Divine." The Cathedral of Saint John the Divine. Accessed July 17, 2021. https://www.stjohndivine.org/visit/history/.

The City Center, NYC. "'Four Brubeck Pieces': Murray Louis Dance Company & the Dave Brubeck Quartet." https://www.youtube.com/watch?v=REdwpR2Z9Nc. 1984.

Wagner, Richard K. "Tacit Knowledge in Everyday Intelligent Behavior." *Journal of Personality and Social Psychology* 52 (6): 1236–1247. 1987.

CHAPTER 7

Dewey, John. *Experience and Education.* New York, NY: The Macmillan Company. 1938.

Experience and Education. 20th ed. New York, NY: Macmillan Publishing. 1977.

Hansen, James R. *First Man: The Life of Neil A. Armstrong.* New York, NY: Simon & Schuster. 2005.

Joy, Rachel. "How Neil Armstrong Avoided Crash Landing on the Moon and Made History Instead." *Florida Today,* July 18, 2019. 2019.

Mission Operations Branch: Flight Crew Support Division. July 31, 1969. *Apollo 11 Technical Crew Debriefing (U).* National Aeronautics and Space Administration (Houston, TX: National Aeronautics and Space Administration). https://www.ibiblio.org/apollo/Documents/Apollo11TechnicalCrewDebriefing-Volume1.pdf. 1969.

National Aeronautics and Space Administration. 1969a. *Apollo 11 Timeline.* National Aeronautics and Space Administration (Houston, TX). https://history.nasa.gov/SP-4029/Apollo_11i_Timeline.htm. 1969

NASA. June 21, 201 1969b. *Apollo 11 Onboard Voice Transcription (U): Recorded on the Command Module Onboard Recorder Data Storage Equipment (DSE).* National Aeronautics and Space Administration (NASA) (Houston, TX). https://history-collection.jsc.nasa.gov/JSCHistoryPortal/history/mission_trans/AS11_CM.PDF. 1969.

Novet, Jordan. "Nancy Pelosi called Zoom 'a Chinese entity,' but it's an American company with an American CEO." CNBC.com. Last Modified August 21, 2021. https://www.cnbc.

com/2020/04/15/nancy-pelosi-calls-zoom-a-chinese-entity.html. 2020.

Plessner, Henning, Cornelia Betsch, and Tilmann Betsch. "Preface." In *Intuition in Judgment and Decision-Making*, edited by Henning Plessner, Cornelia Betsch, and Tilmann Betsch. New York, NY: Taylor & Francis. 2010.

"Meet Eric Yuan, the Founder and CEO of Zoom, Who Has Made over $12 Billion since March and Now Ranks among the 400 Richest People in America." Insider. Last Modified July 31, 2021. *https://www.businessinsider.com/meet-zoom-billionaire-eric-yuan-career-net-worth-life?op=1*. 2020.

Scherer, Douglas. "Levinson's Dream Theory and Its Relevance in an Academic Executive Mentoring Program: An Exploratory Study of Executive Mentors' Practice and Individuation." Ed.D., Organizational Leadership and Learning, Columbia University. 2010.

Soyer, Emre, and Robin M. Hogarth. "Learning from Experience in Nonlinear Environments: Evidence from a Competition Scenario." *Cognitive Psychology* 81 (2015): 48–73. 2015.

Waters, Richard. "Eric Yuan, a Tech Boss Riding a Geopolitical Storm." FT.com. Financial Times. Last Modified July 9, 2020. *https://www.ft.com/content/34055e16-a70a-11ea-92e2-cbd-9b7e28ee6*. 2020.

Wilson, Arthur L., and Elisabeth R. Hayes. "On Thought and Action in Adult and Continuing Education." In *Handbook of Adult and Continuing Education*, edited by Arthur L. Wilson and Elisabeth R. Hayes, 15–32. San Francisco, CA: Jossey-Bass. 2020.

Zoom CEO Eric S. Yuan: How to Manage Customer Experience? In *CxOTalk*: Cambridge Publications. 2021.

CHAPTER 8

Agarwal, Ritu, Daniel Z. Sands, Jorge Díaz Schneider, and Detlev H. Smaltz. "Quantifying the Economic Impact of Communication Inefficiencies in US Hospitals." *Journal of Healthcare Management* 55 (4): 265–281. 2010.

Bollinger, Lee C. "Shailagh Murray Appointed Executive Vice President for Public Affairs." *Columbia University*. September 05, 2018. *https://gca.columbia.edu/news/shailagh-murray-appointed-executive-vice-president-public-affairs*. 2018.

Chapple, Craig. "Pokémon Go Hits $1 Billion in 2020 as Lifetime Revenue Surpasses $4 Billion." Sensor Tower Blog. Sensor Tower. Last Modified July 1, 2021. *https://sensortower.com/blog/pokemon-go-one-billion-revenue-2020*. 2020.

Fogel, Stefanie. "'Pokémon Go' Global Revenue Grew Thirty-Seven Percent in 2018 (Analyst)." *Variety* January 3, 2019.

Institute for Public Relations. "Connecting Organizational Communication to Financial Performance—2003/2004 Communication ROI Study." Institute for Public Relations. Last Modified August 1, 2021. *https://instituteforpr.org/organizational-communication-and-financial-performance/*. 2012.

Langer, Arthur M. *Analysis and Design of Next-Generation Software Architectures: 5G, IoT, Blockchain, and Quantum Computing*. Cham, Switzerland: Springer, 2020.

Machado, Antonio. *Poesías Completas De Antonio Machado*. Madrid, Spain: Publicaciones de la Residencia de Estudiantes. 1917.

Malone, Lesley. *Desire Lines a Guide to Community Participation in Designing Places*. London, England: RIBA Publishing. 2018.

McLuhan, Marshall. *Understanding Media: The Extensions of Man.* CreateSpace Independent Publishing Platform. 2016.

Merriam-Webster. "Desire Line." Merriam-Webster.com dictionary. Last Modified September 6, 2021. *https://www.merriam-webster.com/dictionary/desire%20line.*

Murray, Shailagh. "A Letter from Executive Vice President Shailagh Murray to the Community." *Columbia University.* December 12, 2018.

Nintendo Co, LTD. October 26, 2016. *Consolidate Financial Highlights.* Nintendo (Minami-ku, Kyoto). *https://www.nintendo.co.jp/ir/pdf/2016/161026e.pdf.* 2016.

Reyes-Klann, Joél. "The Road More Traveled: When to Take or Change the Paths of Least Resistance." Matthaei Botanical Gardens and Nichols Arboretum. Last Modified June 20, 2017. Accessed September 5, 2021. *https://mbgna.umich.edu/the-road-more-traveled-when-to-take-or-change-the-paths-of-least-resistance/.* 2017.

Schein, Edgar H. "The Role of the CEO in the Management of Change: The Case of Information Technology." In *Information Technology and the Corporation of the 1990s,* edited by Thomas J. Allen and Schott Morton Michaels. New York, NY: Oxford University Press. 1994.

Schön, Donald. *Beyond the Stable State.* New York: Random House. 1971.

Schorr, Parker. "Desire paths: the unofficial footpaths that frustrate, captivate campus planners." W News. University of Wisconson-Madison. Last Modified September 6, 2021. *https://news.wisc.edu/desire-paths-the-unofficial-footpaths-that-frustrate-captivate-campus-planners/.* 2019.

Sexton, Sarah. "Maryland Images Tour Guides Share What You Might Not Know About the University of Maryland." ULoop. University of Maryland. 2012.

Staeger, Steve. "Desired Paths' May Be the Key to Sidewalks at Some Universities." NBC 9 News. NBC 9 News. https://www.9news.com/article/news/local/next/desired-paths-may-be-the-key-to-sidewalks-at-some-universities/73-557919360. 2018.

Wong, Joon Ian. "We Finally Know How Much Nintendo Made from Pokémon Go." Quartz. Last Modified July 1, 2021. https://qz.com/819677/nintendo-pokemon-go-profits-we-finally-know-how-much-nintendo-made-from-pokemon-go/. 2016.

Yorks, Lyle, Judy O'Neil, and Victoria J. Marsick. "Action Learning: Theoretical Bases and Varieties of Practice." *Advances in Developing Human Resources* 1 (2): 1–18. 1999.

CHAPTER 9

Agnihotria, Raj, and Michael T. Krush. "Salesperson Empathy, Ethical Behaviors, and Sales Performance: The Moderating Role of Trust in One's Manager." *Journal of Personal Selling & Sales Management* 35 (2): 164–174. 2015.

Arenas, Nancy, and Tara Silver-Malyska. "Imagining the Unimaginable: Best Practices for Returning to Work Post-Covid-19." *Benefits Quarterly* 31 (1): 45–56. 2021.

Bellizzi, Joseph A., and Ronald W. Hasty. "Supervising Unethical Sales Force Behavior: How Strong Is the Tendency to Treat Top Sales Performers Leniently?" *Journal of Business Ethics* 43 (4): 337–351. 2003.

Chapin, Tom. Talk About Things That Matter. In *Voices of the Cliff*, edited by Douglas Scherer. Westchester, New York: Douglas Scherer. 2011.

Cooper, Brittney. *Eloquent Rage: A Black Feminist Discovers Her Superpower*. New York, NY: St. Martin's Press. 2018.

Hojman, Daniel A., and Álvaro Miranda. "Agency, Human Dignity, and Subjective Well-Being." *World Development* 101 (2018): 1–15. 2018.

Products by Women. "About Us-Products by Women." Products by Women. Accessed August 1, 2021. https://productsbywomen.com/about-us/. 2020.

Rao-Nicholson, Rekha, Zaheer Khan, and Peter Stokes. "Making Great Minds Think Alike: Emerging Market Multinational Firms' Leadership Effects on Targets' Employee Psychological Safety after Cross-Border Mergers and Acquisitions." *International Business Review*: 103–113. 2016.

Schön, Donald. *Educating the Reflective Practitioner*. San Francisco, CA: Jossey-Bass. 1987.

Winnicott, D. W. *Playing and Reality*. London, UKs: Taylor & Francis. 2017.

Wisdom, Ashlee, "How Healthcare's Failures Fuel Innovation," 2020, in *TEDxWakefield*, https://www.ted.com/talks/ashlee_wisdom_how_healthcare_s_failures_fuel_innovation. 2020.

CHAPTER 10

Covington, David W., and Michael F. Hogan. "Zero Suicide: The Dogged Pursuit of Perfection in Health Care." *Psychiatric Times* 36 (1): 16–17. 2019.

Dass, Ram. *Be Love Now: The Path of the Heart*. New York, NY: HarperCollins. 2010.

Flett, Gordon L., and Paul L. Hewitt. "Measures of Perfectionism." In *Measures of Personality and Social Psychological Constructs*, edited by Gregory J. Boyle, Donald H. Saklofske and Gerald Matthews, 595–618. London, UK: Academic Press. 2015.

Hewitt, Paul l., Carmen F. Carlian, Chang Chen, and Gordon L. Flett. "Perfectionism, Stress, Daily Hassles, Hopelessness, and Suicide Potential in Depressed Psychiatric Adolescents." *Journal of Psychopathology and Behavioral Assessment* 36: 663–674. 2014.

Kabat-Zinn, Jon. *Full Catastrophe Living: Using the Wisdom of Your Body and Mid to Face Stress, Pain, and Illness.* New York, NY: Bantam Books. 2013.

Komori, Shigetaka. *Innovating out of Crisis: How Fujifilm Survived (and Thrived) as Its Core Business Was Vanishing.* Berkeley, CA: Stone Bridge Press. 2013.

Mezirow, Jack. "Learning to Think Like an Adult: Core Concepts of Transformation Theory." In *Learning as Transformation: Critical Perpective on a Theory*, edited by Jack Mezirow and Associates. San Francisco, CA: Josey-Bass. 2000.

Scelfo, Julie. "Suicide on Campus and the Pressure of Perfection." *New York Times* July 27, 2015.

Zero Suicide Alliance. "About Us." Zero Suicide Alliance. Accessed September 5, 2021. *https://www.zerosuicidealliance.com/about/about-us*. 2021.

CHAPTER 11

Armstrong, William Howard. *Study Is Hard Work.* New York, NY: Harper & Brothers. 1956.

Huddleston, Tom, Jr. "A Bill Gates speech inspired Zoom founder to start an internet business—now he's a billionaire." CNBC: Make It. CNBC.com. Last Modified August 3, 2021. *https://*

www.cnbc.com/2019/04/18/zoom-ipo-bill-gates-speech-inspired-founder-to-move-to-us.html. 2019.

Kennedy, John F. "Undelivered Remarks for Dallas Citizens Council, Trade Mart, Dallas, Texas, 22 November 1963." Dallas Citizens Council, Trade Mart, Dallas, TX, November 22, 1963. https://www.jfklibrary.org/asset-viewer/archives/JFKPOF/048/JFKPOF-048-022. 1963.

Konrad, Alex. "Zoom, Zoom, Zoom! The Exclusive Inside Story of the New Billionaire Behind Tech's Hottest IPO." Forbes. Forbes Media. Last Modified August 2, 2021. https://www.forbes.com/sites/alexkonrad/2019/04/19/zoom-zoom-zoom-the-exclusive-inside-story-of-the-new-billionaire-behind-techs-hottest-ipo/?sh=42bde4084af1. 2019.

Mandela, Nelson. *Notes to the Future: Words of Wisdom*. New York, NY: Atria Books. 2012.

Power, Garon. "What Do You Really Need to Wear When You Blacksmith?" *Blacksmithing Basics* (blog), *Blacksmithing Basics*. https://blacksmithingbasics.com/what-do-you-really-need-to-wear-when-you-blacksmith/. 2021.

Waters, Eric Yuan, a Tech Boss Riding a Geopolitical Storm, 2020.

INDEX

Page numbers in italics refer to figures and tables.

A

Accelerated communication, 146-148, *147*t
Action learning, 143
Adapting, 162, 170
Ahn, Kelly, 162–164, 170, 192
Amazon.com, 57–59, 65, 201
Apollo 11, 121–123, *122*f, 129–132
Armstrong, Neil, 121–123, 129–132

B

Barra, Mary, 32–33
Bezos, Jeff, 58–59
Big bang, 55–56, 60
Body awareness, 182
Bootstrapping, 162, 170
Butte County, CA, 91

C

Camp Fire, 91
Chandler, Colby, 62
Chapin, Tom, 157, 174
Clarke, David, 132–137, 192
Cognitive redefinition, 150, 154
Columbia University, 148, 162, 185, 201
Common Fire, 78–79
Compassion, 78–80, 86–90, 159, 162–163, 191–192, 196
Compassion fatigue, 82–83

D

Desire lines / desire paths, 142–143, *143f*
Dewey, John, 126–128
Digital camera, 60–63
Digital Millennium Copyright Act of 1998 (DMCA), 68–69
Disruption, 52–55
Dobbs Ferry Food Pantry, 168–169, 201
Dopamine and the success paradox, 45–46

E

Empathy
    see Compassion

F

F.O.R.G.E.D. acronym, 36–37
Facilitative leader, 49, 199
Flexible thinking, 117–119
Forged leader intuinator, 138, *139t*
Fostering, 161–163, 170
Frank, Sethretta, 95–102
Fujifilm, 62–64, 201

G

Gambale, Virginia, 112–117, 192
General Motors (GM), 32–33, 201
Good enough leadership, 160–161

H

Habit
Habitual behaviors, 46
Habitual responses, 105–106
Health In Her HUE, 165–167, 173, 201
Human-agency, 158–159, 161–163

I

Improvisation, 107, 111–112
Inamdar, Amruta, 177–178, 180–181, 201
Intelligent risk, 124–125, 199
Intuition, 124–127, 137t, 181–182
 see also Forged leader intuinator

J

JetBlue, 115–116, 201

K

Kodak, 60–63, 201
Koletzke, Peter, 107–111, *110*f, 192
Komori, Shigetaka, 63–64, 187
Kortum-Stermer, Jeanie, 78
Kronborg Thomsen, Lotte, 83–86

L

Larkins, Robin, 167–170
LEGO and resilient transformation, 65–70

Leona, Phoebe, 178–180
Li & Fung, 93–94, 102, 202

M

Machado, Antonio, 145–146
Meaning of purpose, 127–132, *128f*, 199
Mindfulness, 180–181, 185–186
MIT Artificial Intelligence Laboratory, 66, 202
Murray Louis Dance Company (MLDC), 108–110, 202
Murray, Shailagh, 148–153, 185
Murthy, Naimeesha, 164–166, 170–172

N

nOMad Collective, 178, 202
nonjudgment, 184–185
Notani, Sunil, 87–90

P

Patience, 185–186
Perfectionism, 184, 186–187
Petraeus, David, 44–45
Pokemon GO, 147–148
Products by Women, 164–166, 202

Q

Quintero, Nélida, 146

R

Resilient change, 56, 60–64, *64f*, 71, 199
Resilient transformation, 57, 65, 69–71, *70f*, 200
Resilient transition, 56–60, *59f*, 71, 200

S

Sasson, Steve, 60
Schein, Edgar, 150–151
Schön, Donald, 144–147, 159
Schreiner, Kathy, 93–95
S-curve, 96–98, 97f, 200
Shanebrook, Robert, 61
Shaw, Beth, 178, 184
Sinek, Simon, 67, 69
Skiles, Jeff, 30–31
Sloan, Julia, 39–43, 42f, 43f
Strategic planning, 39–40
Strategic thinking, 39–42
Success paradox, 45–48, 53–54, 118
Sullenberger, Sully, 29–32

T

Taiano, Marcelo, 167–170
Three Cs, 196
Traditional leader, 49
Transforming aggressiveness, 87

V

Volatile Times, 23, 33–34, 200

W

Winnicott, Donald, 160–161
Wisdom, Ashlee, 164–167, 170–171, 173
Wojak, Angie, 179–180

Y

YogaFit Training Systems Worldwide, 178, 202
Yuan, Eric, 135–137, 191, 194–195

Z

Zoom Video Communications, 202
  see also Yuan, Eric